THE ORMSTOWN DREAM :

Power of the mind Based upon true story 1986-2017

Adam Green

DEDICATION

I would like to dedicate this book to my beloved family,
who has always been there for me.

Contents

Introduction 1

PART 1 3

   CHAPTER 1: The Schoolyard Proclamation and Meeting Jimmy Hilton I'm grateful to say I have a story to portray 3

   CHAPTER 2: Training with Paul Roy: A Mentorship in Speed and Precision 10

   CHAPTER 3: Russ Anber's Gym and Back-to-Back Battles .. 15

   CHAPTER 4: The Quiet Victory of Rehabilitation and Redemption 18

   CHAPTER 5: Intense Training and Tight Bonds: Life on the Quebec Team 20

   CHAPTER 6: From Ormstown to RDS Broadcast 24

PART 2 30

   CHAPTER 7: Impressing the Managers: a Path to the Pros .. 30

   CHAPTER 8: From Amateur to Pro: Shedding the Headgear 32

   CHAPTER 9: Running on Momentum: 3 Fights in 3 Months. 36

CHAPTER 10: Building a Reputation: Making a Name in Montreal 38

CHAPTER 11: Raging Bull, Old Mongoose, and George Chuvalo 41

CHAPTER 12: One Round Blitz and Paul Michaud's Ultimatum. 45

CHAPTER 13: A New G.Y.M. and The Grant Brother's 49

CHAPTER 14: A Clash of Undefeated Records 52

CHAPTER 15: Bonds Beyond Boxing: From Arrogance to Gratitude 54

CHAPTER 16: An Unexpected Challenge. 61

CHAPTER 17: Hope on the Horizon: Battling Internal Turmoil. 64

CHAPTER 18: Plot Twists and Knockouts 68

CHAPTER 19: Mountain Mornings in Sin City. 70

CHAPTER 20: The Cost of Deviation: Sticking to the Game Plan. 72

CHAPTER 21: Taste of Victory: Sweet Success. 78

CHAPTER 22: Friends Turned Foes: Clash of the Titans. 83

CHAPTER 23: The Swing Bout Saga: Waiting in Limbo 90

Part 3: 93

CHAPTER 24: A Fight for Fame and Fortune: The Dave Hilton Jr. Showdown. 94

CHAPTER 25: Taking a Chance: A Bold Move at the Store Counter. 106

CHAPTER 26: Flicker of the Boxing Flame. 113

CHAPTER 27: Return to the Roots: Training with Jimmy Hilton. 116

CHAPTER 28: From Grief to Growth: Transforming Pain into Power. 120

CHAPTER 29: Defying Doubtful Critics: from Inactivity to Intensity. 126

CHAPTER 30: Ring Rust and Redemption: The Final Countdown. 131

CHAPTER 31: The Price of Passion: Sacrifices for the Boxing Dream. 138

CHAPTER 32: A Rocky Road to Recovery: Struggles and Setbacks 145

CHAPTER 33: Twist of fate: A Message from a Matchmaker. 150

CHAPTER 34: Manifesting Dreams into Reality: Mind Over Matter 162

CONCLUSION 173

INTRODUCTION

In 1995 I watcht the Mike Tyson movie, n Instantansly obsest on all the roles n ideas of a boxer must attribute. Cus damato Tyson mentar in tysons beginings for myself cus is the man of all mans when comes to knowledge for up n comer n seesend boxer as well. I watched this movie until everything would be programed in my head I was literly hooked with this movie n that's exactly where I would devolep my desir witch again is 90 percent of this game .Now my mind was possessed n ready to go through it all, the sacrifice the every day in n out process in witch I find myself a little on the crazy side lol, cause honestly I had no idea wat I was getting myself into. Everything happens cause it suppose to, and im am truly grateful in witch I could ekknowledge that it wouldn't be a waste of my time. Listen iam proud jornee only some people would ever be able to withstand this second for none hardest profession I always for some reason been curious with boxers when dad n I would watch aboxing match n I would always be wanting to have a boxers nose for some paticular reason lol. Everything about a boxer bottom line I would be intrigued by these people

Not to long after things would work out the way it was suppose with my bff would introduce me to Jimmy Hilton n from there would all take off from there.

In 2022 I would start putting my ideas in to action just like that I would start to write in my empty note pad. With a lot of reflection n would slowy start to   to joyt down my memmor

This here would be my journee into the sport I was so attached to. Iwould like to thank everyone included, in this n to all the people that who are interested in my boxing book.

Im more than blessed to have experienced all ups n downs this sport has to offer,with always having a mindset that grows continuosly Everything in this book is straight forward n no trying to soffen up any parts.My motto is always to be true to yourself n say it, the way it actuely took place.

Hope u enjoy in wat would be considered my path,in the most intriguing sport there is .

PART 1

CHAPTER 1: The Schoolyard Proclamation and Meeting Jimmy Hilton I'm grateful to say I have a story to portray.

In 1992, aboard the school bus at C.V.R. (Chateauguay Valley Regional High School), I found myself proudly proclaiming to everyone that I was a boxer. Though it wasn't true, there was a flicker of something within me, a vision of what could be. Every Sunday, after my father's hockey games, we'd return home, transforming our basement into a boxing ring. He'd become Larry Holmes, and I, Mike Tyson. This ritual, spanning from 1986 to around 1991, was when it started to unravel. Ladies and gentlemen, this is, and was, the start of my journey in the boxing world.

During the summer of 1995, a pivotal moment occurred when my best friend Jeff Saumier introduced me to Jimmy Hilton, youngest of the five famous Hilton brothers, one of which was a former World Champion. Jimmy would be promoting a boxing gala at the Huntingdon fair, the town next to mine, where I would witness my 1stlive boxing amateur gala. The rumor was that Jimmy was in the process of opening his own gym in the same town and I knew I needed to join and take advantage of life's unique opportunity. I started to box in late '95 and I was in a place

I was destined to be, finding my true path towards success. Jimmy would often take me to the side and say, "You remind me of my brothers, you have what it takes, now it's all up to you". Honestly, I would acquire a sentiment that I would never want to let go of. This made it easier to commit to a daily schedule of training at his gym after school, with 4 other friends.

In May 1996 at the age of 15, I had my first amateur fight in Huntingdon, Quebec, fueled by the cheers of family and friends. The bout was a rollercoaster of overwhelming emotions, resulting in me starting to panic with tears filling my eyes at the end of round two. I looked to Jimmy for support but was met only with him downplaying the situation with his laughter snapping me back to the present moment, igniting a fire of reality within. With determination, I clinched victory with a third-round TKO. However, the closure of Jimmy's gym later that year marked the end of an era.

Enter Jerry Burton, a seasoned ex-boxer and my second trainer with his son and professional boxer, Marty. Jerry's other son Corey was a former Canadian champion in the amateurs. Jerry guided me into my next fight in Thetford Mines, in May 1997 for the Silver Gloves. He was a little older so he would send Marty to work in my corner. My memories of this would be my brother in the morning at the hotel, the day before the fight at the weigh-in, with a big fat joint in his mouth and Marty would humorously state

"What?! Are you a fucking hippie?!". That night, I was honestly petrified and would get maybe a couple hours of sleep due to not being able to rest my mind. I would fight Christian Ouellet, an experienced amateur from Sorel, and I only had one fight under my belt. It was all a blur from the beginning, I was not able to focus in a proper manner and he would end up stopping me in round 1 by TKO. I would even experience my 1st flash knockdown. It was indeed a welcoming of the ups and downs of this viscous sport. Boxing is based on the three words: "Having Ring Experience". I did not understand this at the time and was devastated. This was just the beginning of my long sensible process of humbling wisdom in becoming a boxer.

As time passed, Jeff and I continued our conversations with Jimmy, who had relocated his training to his brother Alex's gym in Ville-Emard. Now 16, I would have my licence and my parents were nice enough to lend me their van. Every day after school, Jeff and I made the daily pilgrimage (an hour each way) to Monk Boulevard, Montreal, to train with the Hilton brothers, Jimmy, Alex, and former world champion, Matthew. It was a period of growth and camaraderie, marked by unforgettable moments in the ring and shared laughter. To be real, I looked up to them and always especially loved to be around Jimmy as he was highly entertaining. There would be an occasion were I spared 1 of Alex's fighters and I dropped him with a good left hook. Jeff would run to the corner with a big smile on his face, trying to hide from Alex, who would be upset about the fact that my gloves were too small. It was at this time that Jeff would be starring in a movie called "THE KID" with Rob Steiger. I had also auditioned, and they wanted me but I was looking more for the final contender part which Stephane Desormiers would be already playing.

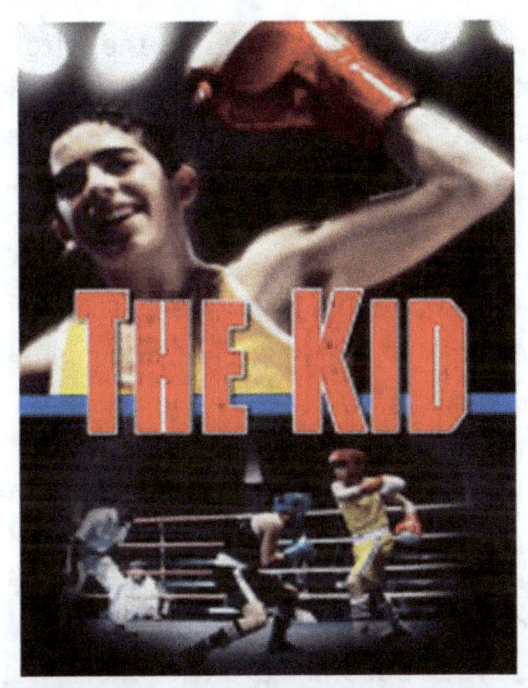

My next fight would be a surprise as the Hiltons, Jeff, and I would attend a boxing gala at the Claude-Robillard Center as spectators. That night, Jimmy got an offer for me to fight Jean Pascal who had an impressive resume behind him already, this was at the end of '97. The good news, it would be an exhibition match, meaning it would automatically have a neutral effect on the boxer's standing while still gaining that in-ring experience. I'm grateful for this opportunity to hone my skills in my third bout against someone seasoned but not having to consider the points. Jean Pascal had a high amount of experience already, having a dozen or so fights. The bottom line is, the more experience you have, the more tricks and knowledge you will accumulate along the way. Each fight, you become a little more relaxed and composed. Again, experience goes a long way in this sport. Bear with me now, I'm boxing Jean Pascal for the first-time and to tell you the truth... I was scared shitless.

I felt like I needed an edge and I tried to intimidate him with one of my tough guy facial expressions, to get inside his head before the fight. But who am I kidding, it's Jean Pascal we're talking about, he showcases one of the strongest mentalities I've ever seen in boxing. Reflecting on that night, I realize I wasn't fully prepared, but I held my own and gave myself a B for effort. It was a lesson learnt in the importance of readiness in the world of boxing. Opportunities come swiftly, and those with the courage and dedication to seize them can rise to greatness. Looking back, I regret my past mentality, but it shaped me into the fighter I am today. To all fighters like me, I extend my respect and admiration for your unwavering dedication and sacrifice to the sport.

CHAPTER 2: Training with Paul Roy: A Mentorship in Speed and Precision

After 6 fights with Jimmy, I took time off from the boxing scene for a couple of months to reflect and assess my current life path. It wasn't until the ice storm of '98 that I found myself watching a historical bout take place: Dave Hilton Jr. vs. Stephane Ouellet. Witnessing that bout was the moment of confirmation I needed to reaffirm my commitment to this path. There's a certain allure to the sport when your trainer is one of the Hilton brothers.

From there, I found myself training at the LaSalle Boxing Club in the basement of the hockey arena. It was there that I crossed paths with Mr. Paul Roy. Our journey together spanned five years, beginning in '98 and lasting until 2003. When we first met, I was a one-dimensional slugger, but Paul saw potential in me that I hadn't yet recognized. I owe him a debt of gratitude for everything he taught me, skills that I utilized throughout my entire career. Paul, I want to take the time to thank you from the bottom of my heart.

Paul Roy was the only trainer I truly enjoyed doing pads with. We developed a system focused on speed and fast combinations; I'm talking 10 to 12 punches at a time. What set Paul apart was his unconventional training methods. Sometimes, our sessions consisted of 15 to 20 rounds of uninterrupted shadow boxing or skipping, followed by intense ab workouts with a medicine ball. I recall Paul always called me champ even long before I was to become one. We would spend a lot of quality time together that I truly cherished. At this moment, he was like my second father and helped guide me in every way to sharpen up my chances of becoming known in this difficult profession.

Paul and I go way back, sharing countless memories. I remember staying at his apartment in Lachine near 10th Avenue, waking up early for runs, and then tagging along on his work trips to Quebec City. Our days were packed with visits to the Fernand Marcotte gym, feasting on chicken at Normandin, and plenty of intense sparring sessions..

Everything had been leading up to my debut at the 1998 Quebec Golden Gloves tournament at 165 lbs. Winning this tournament wasn't just about the trophy—it was my shot at representing my province at the Canadian Olympic Trials. This was my moment, my chance to prove I belonged.

My first and only fight was against Stephane Monast, a tough, bearded biker. They say boxing is 90 percent mental, and that night, I learned just how true that was. I knew I had the better boxing skills, but doubt started creeping in. Then, in the third round, Monast caught me with a left hook that left me dazed on my feet. When the fight continued, he pounced, unloading punches while I just stood there—frozen, unable to react. That's when the referee stepped in and stopped the match.

Just like that, it was over. Once again, I was left devastated and questioning if I truly had what it took to make it in this sport.

Back to the drawing board we went, acknowledging that 165 pounds was perhaps too heavy for my stature. It was a humbling realization, forcing me to reassess my approach and strive for growth. Paul and I doubled our efforts, focusing on refining my technique to become a cleaner boxer with lots of "punches in bunches" with excessive speed.

The following year marked a turning point as I faced off against Jean Pascal's half-brother, Nicholson Poulard, in an exhibition match. Everything Paul had instilled in me began to bear fruit as I showcased newfound abilities, particularly my counterpunching skills. With Paul's guidance, I refined my style, exhibiting impeccable timing and speed while letting my opponent come to me before capitalizing on his mistakes.

Our dedication paid off as we found ourselves in a new gym, surrounded by talented sparring partners like the Lemon brothers, Matthew and Anthony, each offering a unique challenge. Matthew would fight like Muhammed Ali, nice side to side movement popping that jab in between and Anthony loved to stand toe to toe and duke it out. I had them and a few others. To go up in this sport, you must have good sparring and a good trainer. Truly, I was blessed. Despite being undersized for the 165-pound division at barely 5 feet 7 inches, we persevered, focusing on honing different facets of my boxing repertoire.

In May 1999, I entered the Golden Gloves tournament at the Claude-Robillard Center. My opponent, Kenny Ngoto, stood at an imposing 6 feet 2 inches. We had already fought before and I had walked away with the victory, however, this fight would be the important one. While I held my own, the new scoring system worked against me, and despite delivering some solid blows, a standing 8-count from the referee led to a loss by decision.

It was a tough pill to swallow, but in boxing, defeat is part of the journey. I emerged from the experience stronger, determined to rise above adversity. With too many moments of glory to count, I couldn't imagine abandoning the sport that had become such an impact on my life.

Paul and I gathered a pile of victories before we once again collided with Jean Pascal for the second time. It was on the undercard of Hercules Kyvelos vs. Fitz Vanderpool for the Canadian welterweight title on February 15, 2000, at the Molson Center (now the Bell Center in Montreal). I'm not sure if they still do this, but they used to have pro-am cards, featuring both professional and amateur fights. This format provided me with the perfect opportunity to gain exposure and slowly build my reputation as an action-packed boxer.

Despite my belief that I had bested Jean Pascal in our rematch, the judges saw it differently, scoring the fight 7 to 5 in his favor. Even Pascal himself acknowledged to Paul Roy that he had thought the match was mine. It was my introduction to the political landscape of boxing, where sometimes the judges' decisions don't necessarily align with the truth seen by the spectators.

CHAPTER 3: Russ Anber's Gym and Back-to-Back Battles

The new year kicked off with a showdown against Garry Harvey, the reigning Golden Gloves champion at 165. Harvey, known for his heavy hands and crowd-pleasing style, had previously stopped my sparring partner, Matthew Lemon, in spectacular fashion. In our past encounters at the Claude-Robillard Center, I had managed to secure a victory by decision, 6 to 3. This time, the stakes were higher as we clashed in Harvey's hometown of Granby, Quebec.

It was in this fight that I truly began to embody Paul's teachings. He emphasized the importance of "pitter-patter" shots, short punches that may not sound powerful but can inflict significant damage over the course of a bout. The key was to avoid loading up on punches unnecessarily, reserving that power for moments when the opponent was vulnerable. Against Harvey, I put this strategy into practice, gradually wearing him down with precise, calculated shots, much to the surprise of the hometown crowd. It was a defining moment in my amateur career, silencing the audience by the second round.

There was little time to celebrate—I was back in the ring less than 36 hours later, this time facing Sébastien Demers on a Sunday. Demers was a rising talent, tall and lean, with all the makings of a future world-class fighter.

Despite having to weigh in lighter for this bout, I delivered one of the best performances of my amateur career.

By the fourth and final round, I found my rhythm and let loose, unleashing a blistering 10-punch combination, each shot landing flush on Demers' face. In just 48 hours, I had created another defining moment in my journey—one that would stay with me forever.

Paul and I set our sights on dropping down to 156 for the next Golden Gloves tournament. Much of our sparring took place at Russ Anber's gym, a legendary figure in the boxing world. Russ would start off by being Otis's "Magic" Grant's trainer in the 90s eventually guiding him to a world title. He even had his own show on TSN called "In This Corner with Russ Anber" and later created the mega fitness brand "Rival Boxing

Gear". We would have an instant bond; he was even the one who would give me one of my ring names: ADAM GREEN THE ORMSTOWN DREAM. He made me feel good and proud of who I would eventually become. There was one specific time, because I wouldn't have a weight issue at 165lbs, Russ caught me eating a chocolate bar at a trial and said "WHAT THE HELL ARE YOU DOING?! That's what you put in your machine?". Wake up call.

(Russ Anber taking to Paul Roy)

CHAPTER 4: The Quiet Victory of Rehabilitation and Redemption

My third attempt at the Golden Gloves saw me advancing to the second round after defeating my opponent from Longueuil, only to face Jean Pascal for the third time. Despite roughing him up in our previous bout, Pascal showed his ring experience, having represented Canada for the past three years and enjoying government subsidy. His cockiness and arrogance got under my skin, affecting my focus. In the end, I lost according to the judges' decision, acknowledging that he was simply on another level at that time.

The 165lbs final was defined by major drama as the bout between Nicholson Poulard and Kenny Ngoto ended controversially, with both fighters getting disqualified. Though not entirely clear on the details, I believe Ngoto knocked out Poulard after the ref's break call. Bottom line being neither one of them was allowed to represent Quebec, meaning that position was still up for grabs. Meanwhile, my own struggles with drinking

had spiraled out of control, leading me to seek rehabilitation for 21 days following the fight with Jean Pascal.

Rehabilitation was the right move for me, especially for what was about to happen next. I received a call presenting an unexpected opportunity to represent

Quebec at 165lbs. I would need to go through a trial against David Goulet. Known for his previous showdown with Demers in the 147 final, he was a formidable opponent given his crowd-pleasing skills even though he had lost.

Despite having just six days to prepare, i quite smoking immediately I remained determined to seize this chance. The owner of the therapy center allowed my father to bring me my punching bag, which I installed in the shed nearby. Despite being clean and sober, I nevertheless pushed myself through rigorous training.

The day of the fight arrived, and it was unlike any other I had experienced before. With only my people and Goulet's entourage present, along with the judges and the referee, the atmosphere was unusually quiet. So, a very quiet crowd. Though Goulet was expected to be smaller due to his previous weight class, he still appeared larger than me. Despite my less-than-ideal condition, I managed to secure victory over Goulet, but it was clear that I had fought under challenging circumstances.

CHAPTER 5: Intense Training and Tight Bonds: Life on the Quebec Team

Representing Quebec at 165 lbs for the Canadian Trials was a whole new level. Now that I was officially on the Quebec team, I was getting a government stipend to help with training expenses. That meant one thing—I could go all in. No distractions. Just the grind.

Training hit a whole new intensity. I was surrounded by some of Quebec's best—Benoit Gaudet, Sébastien Gauthier, Sébastien Demers, Jean Pascal, my friend Éric Barrak, and super heavyweight David Cadieux. We were a squad, about 12 or 13 of us, living, eating, and training together in a hotel. Everything was structured, every detail locked in. Boxing became life—24/7. No excuses. No shortcuts. Just pure, relentless dedication.

My primary sparring partners were Sebastien Demers and Jean Pascal, now that's efficiency at it's best! This helped me reach peak condition for the trials and bolstered my chances of dethroning the reigning champ, Donnie Orr. "Ken Doll" as I liked to call him. The trials kicked off in Trois-Rivieres, where I secured a comfortable 10-0 victory against my opponent from Manitoba. The following day, facing off against a contender from British Columbia, I claimed another victory with a score of 8-4.

The finals pitted me against Donnie Orr, a former Olympian from BC, and the reigning champion. Pascal even organized a pep rally before my fight with Donnie Orr, a testament to our tight-knit bond. Alongside my close friend and sparring partner Eric Barrak, known for his heavyweight power and colorful personality, boxing became my top priority as I embraced the opportunities for growth that lay ahead. If you've noticed, there were two boxers from BC and this is because the champion doesn't count as a provincial representative as they are considered national. Despite my best efforts, including what I believed to be a winning performance, the judges awarded the victory to Donnie Orr. Nonetheless, I was proud of my journey, especially considering my relatively low number of fights (30) compared to many of my opponents who had 100 fights or more.

Ranked number two in Canada, I still had a chance to face Orr again in another trial, this time it would be held in Sarnia, Ontario. Training remained rigorous, but the camaraderie and structured regimen made it more manageable. Still always partnered up with my buddy Eric Barrak, he would be the character that I loved to be around. Sorry to disappoint anyone but I find it hilarious when there was one time that Barrak barged into a teammates room and he decided to use their restroom, as the kids would all scream "noooo!" with a big smile on their face. Well, he's a bit of a bully and does what he wants whenever he wants.

That night after beating the Ontarian in my preliminary round, I returned to my hotel room. Supposedly resting, my partner and roommate Barrak decides to bring a lady to our room. Without any details, I'll just say women weaken legs, not a profitable decision. Especially since I would have an important fight the next day vs Jason Williams from Alberta. The match was fiercely contested, with both sides giving their all for four rounds. In the end, Williams emerged victorious with a narrow score of 30-29, earning the opportunity to challenge Orr for the Canadian crown instead of myself. Despite the setback, the prevailing sentiment remained that I was undersized for the 165-pound division, but I remained undeterred in my pursuit of success.

I made the decision to rededicate myself to the 156-pound weight class, recognizing that addressing my weight issue, due to my height, was essential to improving my prospects in the sport. With Jean Pascal holding the Canadian championship at 156 pounds, the possibility of having two representatives from Quebec was tantalizing.

However, achieving this would require another attempt at the golden gloves, marking my fourth attempt. I was hungry to win.

In my first fight back at 156 pounds, I secured a victory, setting the stage for what was to come. My next opponent was a skilled young fighter, but I had the advantage of experience on my side. With determination, I entered the ring and emerged victorious, stopping him in the third round.

With this achievement, I solidified my position as a representative of Quebec at 156 pounds. One of the perks of this recognition was having my food expenses covered, a favorite aspect for sure. Additionally, I got to retain the privilege of sparring with Jean Pascal and Sebastian

Demers. Both of whom I held in high regard for their unwavering support.

CHAPTER 6: From Ormstown to RDS Broadcast

It was a bit disheartening to realize that the last Jeux de Francophonie had been held in Madagascar while mine was held in the far away lands of Ottawa. However, my journey continued as I faced my first opponent, who had traveled all the way from South Africa. I secured a peaceful victory with a score of 15 to 2.

The atmosphere shifted when my next opponent was announced – none other than Mr. Jean Pascal himself. The mental aspect of facing Pascal was different, especially after Quebec's contender Sebastien Gautier's upset victory against Benoit Gaudet, one of Canada's top contenders. This would be our fourth matchup and the upset that just happened must've had him thinking. While not possessing the cleanest style in my opinion, he certainly had the brainpower that made him a legend as of today.

I consider my bout with Pascal, which was televised on RDS broadcasted by Yvon Michel, to be one of my best fights as an amateur, even ranking it above my match with Demers. The scoring throughout the rounds was tight:

	Round #1	Round #2	Round #3	Round #4
Adam Green	2	4	7	7

Jean Pascal 1 5 9 15

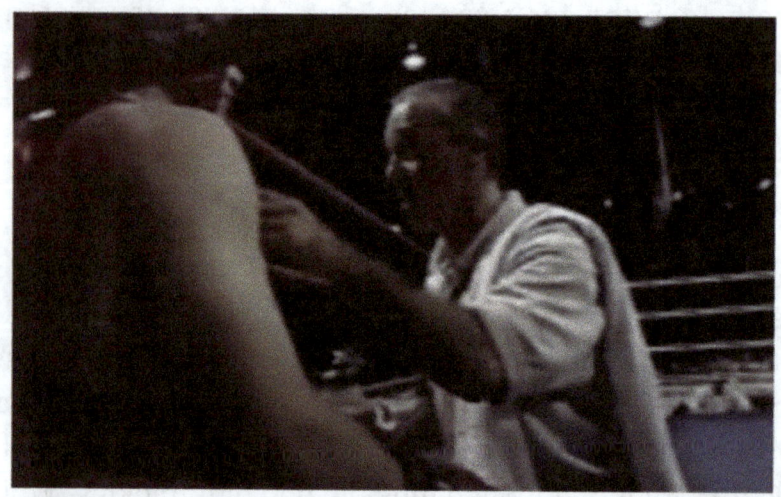

Honestly, I'm still a little resentful that I wasn't awarded at least one point in the 4th round, but the judge's decisions are final and what ultimately decide the outcome. Check out the video for yourself and come to your own conclusion. I maintained a limited patience with boxing, knowing that turning professional was on the horizon.

Proudly transitioning into the professional ranks, I reflected on my achievements as an amateur – ranked second in Canada at 165 pounds, despite facing controversial decisions along the way. My encounters with Pascal, four in total, were notable, along with winning the Golden Gloves in 2001 at 156 pounds. I also had memorable bouts against Renan St. Juste and Sebastian Demers, both of whom have made their mark in the professional boxing world. Coming from Ormstown and starting my journey at the age of 15, I was ready to take on the challenges and opportunities that awaited me in the professional realm.

I would like to thank my dad, Mr. Barry Green, for always filming my fights as an amateur and being my number 1 supporter. His unwavering encouragement means the world to me. I'm truly grateful to have him in my life. THANK YOU, DAD, I LOVE YOU.

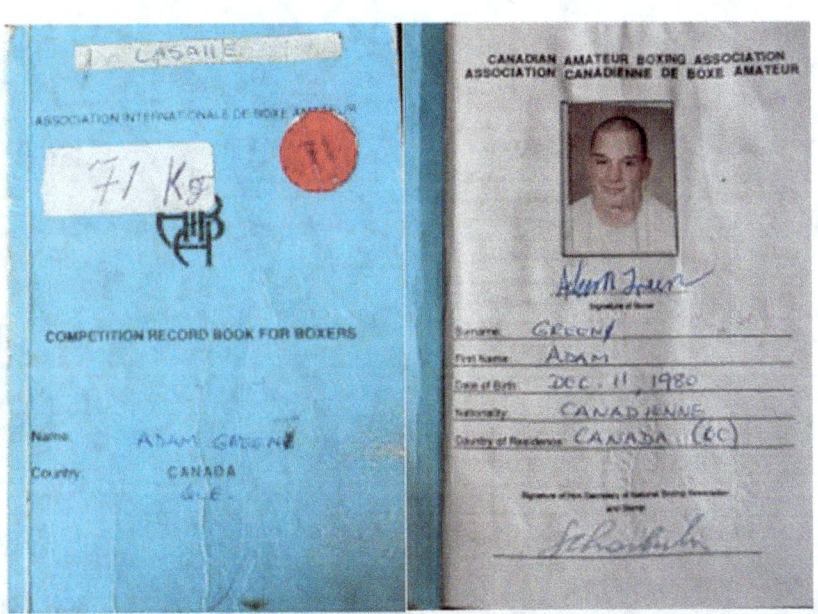

RECORD OF BOUTS

GREENE

Bout NO	Date	Organizer	City	Opponent	Country	Bout Won in Rd.	Lost in Rd.	Ø	Decisions and Comments	Signature by Technical Delegate
17	05 fev 2000	Legend	MTL	Kaiway Ngoto		3			3-3 13-17	
18	15/02 2000	Ons A.M.	MTL	Jean Heynester Garcia			4		D 12-8	DB
19	20/2 2000	Chauvt	MTL	Gus Bazil Lezardo		4			V 2-3	
20	26-02 2000	Gaut Doré	MTL	Kenny angaote			4		4-15	
21	13-10-00	F.Q.B.O	Granby	Garry Harvey		4			39-18	
22	15-10 00	Michel Nox.N	Joliette	Sebastien Demers		4			50-34 Ø V	AF
~~23~~	11/4/00		Morristown, N.J.	Said Ouali			4			LOdebhim
24	11-11-00	FaBe	U.S.A	Ronan St-Jusse		3			V. 22-10	YR
25	25-11-00	F.Q.B.O QUALIF	Victo	Eric Francoeur		4			V 15-7	
26	26-11-00	F.Q.B.O QUALIF	Victo	Jean-T. Pascal			4		D 42-17	KP
27	17-01 2001	F2BO	3.Riv.	David Goulet		4			V 37-26	

PART 2

CHAPTER 7: Impressing the Managers: a Path to the Pros

As Dave Hilton Sr. began training Stephan Ouellet, I found myself in the ring sparring with yet another icon. Our first sparring session went remarkably well, catching the attention of Erick Cliche and Eric Lamontagne, who served as Ouellet's managers. They were highly impressed with my performance against Ouellet, laying the groundwork for my transition into the realm of professional prizefighting. With the necessary paperwork signed, I officially became a professional boxer under the management of KManagement.

Summer of 2001 brought about Ouellet's attempted comeback under the tutelage of Dave Hilton Sr. Despite my initial success in our first session, Ouellet soon reminded me of his caliber as our subsequent sessions began to tilt in his favor. This was Stephane Ouellet everyone, a boxer who had faced Alex Hilton twice and had a historic bout with Dave Jr. during the ice storm in 1998, serving as a pivotal moment in my journey. It was witnessing fights like these that initially inspired me to pursue boxing and I was proud to add him to my ring experience resume.

Reflecting on the Hilton brothers, Dave Jr. had also achieved world champion status in 2001 making him the second Hilton brother to do so. However, his path took a different turn as he faced legal troubles and was sentenced to five years in prison. The contrast of triumph and adversity within the Hilton family added another layer of complexity to my own journey into the professional boxing world.

CHAPTER 8: From Amateur to Pro: Shedding the Headgear

My professional debut was scheduled in Niagara Falls, New York, on October 12th, 2001. Set on the undercard of Donovan "Razor" Ruddock, who had famously fought Mike Tyson twice in 1991 and had given him a run for his money. The exposure on his card was invaluable. My fight, slated as the first of the night, even made it to pay-per-view, serving as a preview before viewers would have to pay. Could not complain one bit!

However, it was a surreal moment, returning from my morning run to find my mother, like many others, in disbelief as the chaotic events of September 11th unfolded on TV. The collapse of the World Trade Center due, turned the world upside down and would cast a shadow over my upcoming professional debut.

October 12, 2001, marked the fight night. My opponent, John Spell from Pittsburgh, Pennsylvania, may have had a record of 1 win, 4 draws, and 5 losses, but in the realm of professional boxing, one mustn't underestimate anyone by their record alone. Bottom line is that he already had 10 fights under his belt as a professional while I was still going through all the emotions of a debut fight. This gala held historical significance as the first-ever Canadian title fight contested outside of the nation, adding another layer of intensity to the bout.

Walking to the ring, emotions ran high. The internal battle with nerves was real, but I repeated to myself: *mind over matter.*

"*This could make you,or break you, you know. Stay calm Adam. Sharp crisp short combinations, stay focused. You can do it Adam, come on! Mind over matter Adam, you can do it champ. Believe in yourself, you've got to be proud doing this Adam. I'm doing this, omfg I'm doing this!*"

The transition from amateur to professional meant no more headgear or shirts. This realization hit me as my hands, now wrapped tight as a rock, awaited their professional debut. With my trainer Paul Roy and the two Erics from KManagement behind me, I entered the ring, determined to make my mark.

The fight against John Spell was intense, with moments of doubt and determination intertwining. In the end, I emerged victorious by majority decision, marking my first professional win and breaking the ice in my career. Celebrating with seasoned Manitoban boxer Chad Brisson, I couldn't help but admire his battle-worn gladiator face with his scars and bulgy eyes. I even jokingly aspired to have a face like his one day.

Adam Green

14 (7 KOs)   **8** (4 KOs)   **0**

division	middle
status	inactive
bouts	22
rounds	122
KOs	50%
career	2001-2017
debut	2001-10-12

ID#	069476
sex	♂ male
nationality	🇨🇦 Canada
stance	orthodox
height	5' 7" / 170cm
residence	🇨🇦 Montreal, Quebec, Canada
wiki	W

✅ 2015-05-22	161½	Francesco Cotroni	161½	10 4 1	●●●●●○	🇨🇦 Colisée Isabelle Brasseur, Saint-Jean-sur-Richelieu	W-SD	6/6
						ref: Steve St Germain Richard DeCarufel 57-56 Nicolas Esnault 57-56 Jean Gauthier 56-57		
✅ 2007-05-01	156½	Dave Hilton	156½	40 2 2	●●●●●●	🇨🇦 Maurice Richard Arena, Montreal	L-UD	10/10
						ref: Marlon Wright Richard DeCarufel 91-98 Pasquale Procopio 92-97 Jack Woodburn 91-98		
✅ 2006-06-23	162½	Stephan Boyd	162½	7 2 0	●●●●●●	🇨🇦 Uniprix Stadium, Montreal	L-TKO	3/6
						⏱ 2:40 ref: Jean Guy Brousseau Richard DeCarufel Robert Gay Claude Paquette		
✅ 2006-04-26	153½	Stephane Desormiers	153½	13 1 0	●●●●●●	🇨🇦 Metropolis, Montreal	L-1KO	10/10
						⏱ 1:48 ref: Gerry Bolen Richard DeCarufel Claude Paquette Pasquale Procopio		
✅ 2006-02-02	156	Claudio Ortiz	156½	6 10 0	●●●●●●	🇨🇦 Metropolis, Montreal	W-UD	8/8
						ref: Michael Griffin Richard DeCarufel 78-71 Robert Gay 79-70 Jean Lapointe 80-69		
✅ 2005-11-02	146⅝	Victor Lupo Puiu	146½	9 0 1	●●●●●●	🇨🇦 Metropolis, Montreal	L-UD	10/10
						ref: Marlon Wright Richard DeCarufel 89-100 Pasquale Procopio 91-98 Jack Woodburn 91-98		

● 2005-07-13	163½	Frankie Sanchez	169½	13 14 1	●●●●●●	🇨🇦 Metropolis, Montreal	W-TKO	5/10
					⏱ 3:00 ref: Gerry Bolen Richard DeCarufel Claude Paquette Dale Suddaby			
● 2005-03-03	151½	Justin Danforth	146½	4 3 0	●●●●●●	🇨🇦 Club Soda, Montreal	W-TKO	5/6
					⏱ 0:40 ref: Gerry Bolen Sylvain Leblanc Benoit Roussel Dale Suddaby			
● 2004-12-17	155	Alex Hilton	158½	37 10 0	●●●●●●	🇨🇦 Bell Centre, Montreal	W-TKO	6/8
					⏱ 1:38 ref: Michael Griffin Richard DeCarufel Claude Paquette Jack Woodburn			
● 2004-11-03	154¾	Matt O'Brien	155½	8 0 0	●●●●●●	🇨🇦 Club Soda, Montreal	L-UD	6/6
					ref: Gerry Bolen Richard DeCarufel 56-58 Jean Lapointe 56-58 Pasquale Procopio 56-58			
● 2004-09-29	156¾	Ali Nestor Charles	159	4 2 0	●●●●●●	🇨🇦 Club Soda, Montreal	W-UD	6/6
					ref: Gerry Bolen Richard DeCarufel 60-55 Jean Lapointe 60-54 Claude Paquette 60-54			
● 2003-09-12	154	Tyrone Winckler	155¾	12 7 1	●●●●●●	🇺🇸 Blue Horizon, Philadelphia	W-TKO	1/6
					Lynne Carter George Hill Richard Hopkins Jr			
● 2002-10-26	153½	David Goulet	153½	debut		🇨🇦 Le Medley, Montreal	W-UD	4/4
					ref: Marlon Wright 40-35 40-35 40-35			
● 2002-07-09	152½	Sacha Wilner	146½	0 2 0	●●	🇨🇦 Pierre-Charbonneau Centre, Montreal	W-TKO	2/4
					⏱ 2:19 ref: Gerry Bolen			
● 2002-04-26	154½	Jason Diamond	157	1 2 0	●●●	🇨🇦 Hershey Centre, Mississauga	W-UD	4/4
					ref: Dave Dunbar William Boodhoo 40-36 Alan Davis 40-36 Kelly Zolnierczyk 40-36			

CHAPTER 9: Running on Momentum: 3 Fights in 3 Months.

With my debut victory behind me, I was eager to continue my journey. For my second professional fight, I traveled to Mississauga, Ontario, accompanied once again by Mr. Paul Roy and the Erics. I had the expertise of Russ Anber as my cut man, a legend in his own right in the boxing world.

February 1st, 2002.

It is worth mentioning again how Russ Anber's name carries weight. He guided Otis Grant to a world title in the '90s and is now a prominent figure as the owner of Rival Boxing Gear. His skill in wrapping hands for maximum impact and protection was unmatched, an essential asset in the heat of battle. I was facing off against Steve Cormier from Nova Scotia who actually trained at the same gym as me in Lasalle and was making his pro debut. I secured another win with a unanimous decision, maintaining my undefeated record at 2-0.

A month later, KManagement flew me out to my next bout in Long Island, New York, still only six months after the tragic events of 9/11. After the weigh-in (which is held the day prior to the fight) I walked through the streets of New York City with Eric Cliché and the gravity of the situation was palpable, a surreal and somewhat frightening experience.

March 2nd, 2002, saw me back in the ring, this time signed for 157 lbs, aiming to maintain my weight limit. Facing my opponent, I secured my first knockout victory in the second round, bringing my record to an impressive 3-0 with 1 knockout.

With no time to waste and running off momentum, we returned once more to Mississauga for my fourth fight (3rd in 3.5 months). In Jason Diamond, I faced a rugged opponent who put me to the test. Despite Diamond's toughness, I emerged victorious with a unanimous decision after four rounds. While making a name for myself in Mississauga was important, I felt drawn back to Montreal, where I aimed to further establish myself in the boxing scene.

CHAPTER 10: Building a Reputation: Making a Name in Montreal

Between fights, I had a chance to venture into the States once more with my brother Josh. Our border crossing turned into an unexpected adventure when we got denied entry because I mentioned we were going to make some money. It's a funny story we still reminisce about to this day.

My fifth professional fight took place in Montreal at Centre Pierre Charboneau on July 9th, 2002. It was considered a tune-up fight to bolster my record, facing Sacha Wilner whom I stopped in the second round. Despite the perceived ease of the match, I remained cautious and focused, recognizing the unpredictability of the sport. In boxing, you should never underestimate anyone with two fists and a heartbeat.

With each fight, I began to make a name for myself in Montreal, showcasing the qualities of a potential champion. At 22 years old, boasting a professional record of 5 wins, 0 losses, and 2 knockouts, I had the charisma, arrogance, and most importantly, the killer instinct necessary to entertain and succeed in the ring.

Moving on to my sixth pro bout at the Medley in Montreal on October 26th, 2002, I maintained my activity in the ring while balancing work as a telemarketer with Jimmy Hilton. Living in Laval with Jimmy and his girlfriend, I found joy in his lively and entertaining company, often indulging in some drinks and adventures, including a memorable two-day journey to Chateauguay where I met my second girlfriend, Caroline.

Outside of boxing and work, I cherished the time spent with my grandfather, Jimmy Tibour Kellerman, a Czechoslovakian Jew who survived the horrors of World War II at 9 years of age. His infectious humor and warm-hearted nature made him a beloved figure in my life, and our outings for steak dinners on the St. Lawrence were cherished memories. I was fortunate enough to be able to stay at his place in Montreal whenever I needed.

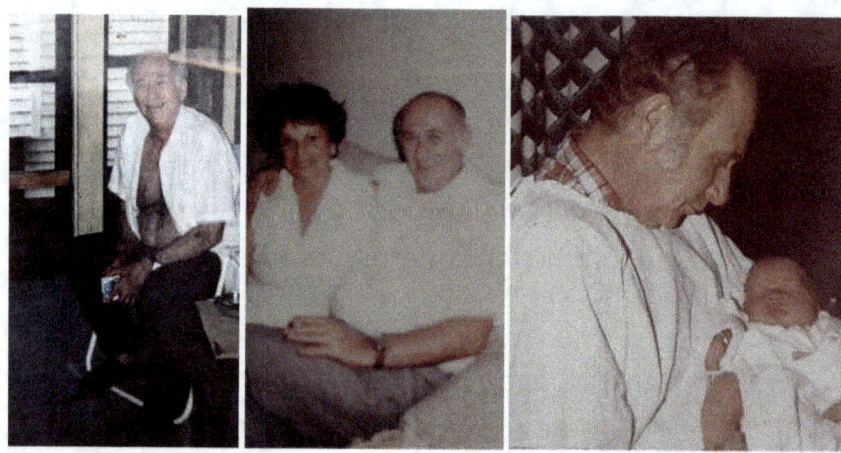

As I prepared for my upcoming bout against Goulet, I remained loyal to my trainer, Paul Roy, at our home gym in LaSalle. However, for sparring sessions, I frequented Mr. Hilton's gym on Monk Boulevard, where I had the privilege of training with formidable partners like Wayne, Aart, and my buddy the late Yan Stanford. We also trained at

Spard gym. Mr. Hilton's expertise in boxing played a pivotal role in my development, and I'm forever grateful to be a part of his team, after all I'm convinced that he's the reason that I have a story to tell you today.

CHAPTER 11: Raging Bull, Old Mongoose, and George Chuvalo

On October 26, 2002, at the Medley in Montreal, I faced off against David Goulet, the only fighter that I ever fought as an amateur and as a professional. As I stepped into the ring, Paul Roy and Mr. Hilton Sr. prepared me for battle, wrapping my hands and serving as my cut man. Goulet was no pushover; he hailed from a family of fighters, and this match would mark my last scheduled four-rounder as a professional. The objective is to slowly build your record by facing opponents selected to help you grow, at the same time adding in the rounds until you get to 10 or 12. This is the best plan but not always easy to execute. In the end, people cross your path unexpectedly through timing and circumstances. Your best bet would be to roll with the punches and do what is most important, by putting yourself in peak condition. This helps increase your chances by displaying a show of the night, always keeping the goal of leaving the crowd in a frenzy saying "WOW! I'm paying anything to come see this boy fight again.".

In the end, I secured the win with a unanimous decision, bringing my professional record to 6 wins and 0 losses with 2 knockouts. Goulet proved to be a formidable opponent, demonstrating the true spirit of a fighter. It was Caroline's first live professional fight experience, and she was thoroughly entertained by the spectacle.

Caroline attending her first live professional fight, I'm reminded of my first live boxing match watching Dave Hilton Jr. face off against Hughes Daigneault on October 22, 1996. Witnessing the electrifying atmosphere and Dave's skill in the ring solidified my desire to pursue boxing. It was a grand moment that set me on the path I continue to walk today. Jimmy Hilton would get Jeff and I into this fight for free and I would be blown away by the electricity in the crowd. When Dave would make his way to the ring, I knew this was it, this is what I wanted to do. Dave would end up scoring a 2nd round knockout, leaving Hughes Daigneault on his knees with blood gushing out of his nose with his head tilted to the ground. Davy Jr is a piece of art in the ring, a true natural for his profession. When I was training with Jimmy from 1996 to 1998, Jeff and I would witness a couple of his brother's fights, mostly Alex and Dave fighting. I was fortunate enough to have witnessed Alex Hilton vs Stephane Ouellete twice and at their 2ndfight, there would be a spectacle at ringside. There seemed to be some confusion with the tickets, and I was upset to not be at ringside with Jimmy. I would proceed my way down to ringside to confront him, we would exchange words and it would finish off with him cracking me with a good shot. In attendance was Jake "Raging Bull" LaMotta, Archie "The Old Mongoose" Moore, and George Chuvalo was the one who actually got in between Jimmy and I.

Caroline and I embarked on a new chapter together, moving into our first apartment in Chateauguay. I juggled my boxing career with work as an assistant chef in Ile-des-Soeurs, where I honed my skills in preparing elegant dishes. Cooking had always been a passion of mine, though I once attempted to pursue a formal culinary education. However, my focus inevitably shifted back to boxing, where my heart truly lay.

As I navigated through these experiences, I parted ways with KManagement, as they had different priorities beyond the realm of boxing. Despite the changes, my love for both boxing and cooking remained unwavering, shaping the journey that lay ahead.

CHAPTER 12: One Round Blitz and Paul Michaud's Ultimatum.

Between fights, it was Paul Roy who orchestrated my next bout connecting me with the famous promoter Don Elbaum. The match against Tyrone Winckler was my favourite fight in the States. It was held at the legendary Blue Horizon in Philadephia, a great historic boxing venue built in 1865 which was one of the filming locations for the fifth Rocky movie. Caroline, Paul, and I made the journey in my parents' van, and what I remember most was once again I could not rest my mind. I was a pack of nerves and wouldn't sleep. Kind of scary knowing you're going into combat, and you didn't get any rest the night before. This is where the power of the mind must come into play.

The gloves were tight and compact when I put them on. The first thing that came to my mind was "someone is going to get hurt and it's not gonna be me.". We're in the states now where things are a little different and since I was in his hometown, he should have the upper hand. That night, I would achieve my fastest KO in round #1.

With this victory, I maintained my undefeated record, standing at 7 victories in 7 fights with 3 knockouts. However, almost a year had passed since my last fight, and it would be another year before my next one. During this hiatus, I continued working at Chaz restaurant in Ile-des-Soeurs while training at Mr. Hilton's gym. It was there that I crossed paths with Jean-Marc Emond. J-M would be the son of "Ti-Guy" Emond, for all the Quebecers out there, he was an entertainer/boxing analyst. J-M knew of a man with a passion for boxing and lots of money, Paul Michaud. To get to the higher ranks of boxing, passion as well as financial backing become important to make it possible to meet the dedication required to ascend.

Paul Michaud became impressed during a sparring session at Mr. Hilton's gym and wanted to be my second manager under his terms. I agreed and we struck a deal. In compliance with the terms of the agreement, I transitioned to training under the Grant Brothers at Club Champion Gym in Montreal owned by George Cherry. Living with Caroline in Chateauguay, we moved to a larger apartment, providing a solid foundation for our respective careers. Caroline was now a flight attendant traveling up North to Kuujjuaq and returning the same day. I was a full-time professional boxer with a 7-0 record. My mind was now set and ready for my destination.

My daily routine was to wake up, have breakfast, leave the apartment in Chateauguay at 9am to be at the gym in Saint-Michel, Montreal for 10am, for rigorous training with prominent boxing professionals like Otis Grant, Adonis Stevenson and Joachim Alcine.

Partners like Stephane Desormiers and Walid Smichet brought out the best in me, pushing me to hone my skills. When Walid, who was originally from Tunisia, and I would put the gloves on, there was non-stop action and entertainment. People would gather in crowds in front of the ring, not believing what they were witnessing and craving more. Howard Grant would say "I'm going to have to start charging people" with a big grin on his face. Being on the same team, we would train together for the next 2 years. We had very similar styles and approaches, with that killer instinct and the will to win. I believe he had the harder punch, but I would have better boxing skills. I can just imagine the number of times we stepped into the ring in those 2 years. We would go into full combat like two viscous gladiators! When I find myself in this type of situation, it's better to switch up your fighting styles and show a different side. It's hard to go to war for 5 or 6 straight rounds which is why you must learn other aspects of this sport. Basically, the goal would be to rest and at the same time popping a jab to the head and body. However, Howard knew that too much punishment is not good for anyone, so in summer of 2004 our goal was not only to prepare for upcoming fights but also to diversify our fighting styles. This period marked a crucial phase in my career as I geared up for what lay ahead.

CHAPTER 13: A New G.Y.M. and The Grant Brother's

Rumors swirled about the Grant Brothers opening their own gym, and soon enough, it became a reality in the West Island, just off Boulevard des Sources.

I vividly remember our initial training sessions in the new gym. Despite its emptiness, we had the most crucial tool for boxing: the ring itself. With the Grant Brothers backed by the biggest boxing promoter Canada has ever produced; Yvon Michel, this was my chance to shine. I knew I had to impress Yvon in my upcoming fight.

On September 29th, 2004, I was scheduled to fight Renan St. Juste, a significant name in boxing whom I had defeated twice in the amateurs. However, the fight fell through, and Charles Ali Nestor stepped in as my opponent. During training, I met Adam Harris and Ian MacKillop, both of whom would have a profound impact on my career.

Fight night arrived at Club Soda, televised on the Vox network. It had been a year since my last fight, and I was anxious about any ring rust. Nestor's southpaw stance posed a challenge, but I applied constant pressure, never allowing him a moment's respite. Always stuck to him like glue and banging hard to his head but mostly his body. I had a nice crowd with good support. I would go the distance for the 1sttime in my career 6 hard fought rounds.

With this win, I signed up with GYM (Groupe Yvon Michel), marking the true beginning of my boxing career. Over the next two years, I would be incredibly active in the ring. While my manager couldn't attend the fight due to prior commitments, Adam Harris was present and impressed. Our bond was instant, and we would become close over the following years.

Adam Harris, just a couple years older than I, would eventually be promoted alongside Yvon Michel. It would be called the "Real Fighting Irish Boxing Promotions" which comes in handy since my last name is Green. I find it humorous that it doesn't matter the fact that I'm of Italian, Jewish, and Danish descent... we're all Irish on St. Patrick's Day anyway. It's all a show and that's what counts. Adam and I would have an instant bond and would remain close friends for the next couple of years to come. I'm blessed to have crossed paths with you Adam, I love you and thank you from the bottom of my heart for all that you have done for me. It's out of my power but I have the impression you felt like I didn't give it my best. You are more than welcome to feel that way, with no hard feelings on my part. Like so many boxers, I had a lot going on at that time regarding injury management, a grueling training regime, and maybe the least discussed but effects boxers the most- life outside the ring. Remember that everyone has different shoes to walk in, with different circumstances. It's not just the fighting we do, it's everything that comes with it. The injuries during training happen all the time, and yes there have been times where I go into a fight with an injury or with troubled thoughts. Thats why this profession is 90 percent in your mind. Peace, love, and respect brother, always.

Ian MacKillop, another influential figure, became a friend and training partner. Little did I know then, he would play a crucial role in the latter stages of my career. Each encounter and connection in the boxing world shaped my journey, teaching me invaluable lessons about respect, perseverance, and the true essence of this profession.

CHAPTER 14: A Clash of Undefeated Records

Standing with a record of 8 wins and 3 KOs, my next bout would prove to be unforgettable. I faced off against Matt O'Brien from Calgary, boasting a record of 8 wins and 4 KOs, both of us mirroring an undefeated record really adding pressure and hype to this highly anticipated bout.

During training, I pushed myself to the limit in every sense. Most likely my mentality was my weak point. Basically, I trained hard with no sense of mercy for myself, which would not be the right way as everyone is human. Maybe some fighters can go all out the whole way, but most of us cannot. Understanding your body during the heat of the battle is crucial and you must acquire the experience to know how to rest and fight. Remember now people, 90 percent of this sport is in the mind, and I know most of you are probably saying bullshit, but It's said for a reason of course. It is up to the individual to accept the reality.

Now as the 1stround would start, I was on fire, and I wanted to let Matt O'Brien know exactly who he was dealing with. I would own the 1stround but, in the 2nd, Matt began to make a statement of his own. Despite knocking him down at the 2:30 mark, the referee called it a slip. Sometimes getting knocked down can switch the momentum and turn the tables around. This forced me to think on the fly. With one round a piece, heading into the 3rd. I would win the 3rdround, but O'Brien would get the edge in the later rounds. Learned a lot in this fight, I think the difference would be the fact that he had more than 60 fights as an amateur compared to my 37 bouts. Again, more ring experience.

While it was my first defeat as a professional, I accepted it with grace, understanding that it was part of the journey toward wisdom, knowledge, and ring experience. Every lesson learnt would shape my future fights, making me a better boxer. This match would go down in Canadian history as the Fight of the Year of 2004. Despite fighting with all my heart, it wasn't enough to sway the judges. Interestingly enough it was becoming clear that Groupe Yvon Michel's "BoxeRock" events were beginning to draw crowds larger than what Club Soda could accommodate, hinting towards the end of boxing events at this venue.

CHAPTER 15: Bonds Beyond Boxing: From Arrogance to Gratitude

My next fight, ladies and gentlemen, would be my most significant yet. Titled "The Changing of the Guards," it pitted me against my early idol, Alex Hilton. Alongside Mike Tyson, the Hilton brothers had been my inspiration when I began my career.

Going back in time now to 1994, I used to play soccer in the summer and hockey in the winter. One winter during my hockey games in Beauharnois, before the game I would go upstairs with my dad to get a drink or something. On the TV would be a boxing match where my dad would say, "look Adam, that's one of the Hilton's". That's where I would develop an attachment to the Hilton name and began envisioning myself as a boxer. Not too long after I would even abandon my two favorite sports to give boxing a shot. Where in hockey I was good but with soccer I would be even better, representing "Quebec Sud-Ouest", an all-star team made up of the best players from the Chateauguay valley. This passion for soccer may have been, in part, from my uncle Caesar who was a semi professional soccer player, from Columbia. He was my coach and gave me the chance to see many live matches which were astounding. He even brought our whole team to Florida to have a few matches as "Canada vs Miami". My cousin Andreas was in the team and would be my best friend growing up since we were only 1 year apart.

Tragically, Caesar would later get shot, in Bogota Colombia, at age 48 in 2002.

Now back to present time for my biggest challenge yet!

Held just before the main event between Joachim Alcine and Stephane Ouellette, our bout took place at the Bell Center on December 17th, 2004, in front of a crowd of 9000 spectators. I faced off against Alex, who had an impressive 48 professional fights under his belt, not to mention countless amateur bouts. It was clear he was nearing the end of his career, but in boxing, there's no room for sympathy.

Adam Green, Professional: 8-1 (3KOs) Amateur: approximately 36 fights Alex Hilton, Professional: 37-11 (23KOs) Amateur: 104-1 (90KOs)

The night had come, and this would be my 3rdfight of the year and second within 6 weeks when I suffered my first loss. This bout would be against a guy I looked up to, could you believe it. I had a hard time wrapping my head around what was about to take place. The emotions were intense, let me tell you and I'll admit, I might have had trouble staying focused.

This would not be a fight with Yvon Michel nor Adam Harris. In contrary it would be with the one and only Mr. Regis Levesque, another big promoter in Montreal. Mr.

Levesque would be more reasonable for your purses when it came to your fight, just saying. Fighting for Mr. Levesque came with a lot more publicity as I would be mentioned in *Journal de Montreal* on multiple occasions.

I recall I didn't do any sparing for this fight as I was suffering from a slight injury to my right bicep. For the past couple of months, I had been more active than usual, but also began finding a good balance between giving your body and brain a break at times, while working on other aspects of boxing. There are always alternative ways of training for every situation. That's exactly what Howard (Grant) and I would pursue, especially since my last fight with O'Brien was only a month ago, and it was a war.

To be fair to my health, I could have easily taken off 6 months. However, I was young, having just turned 25. I felt if I was to throw away this opportunity that was given to me, basically I wouldn't be able to go on with my life. It's hard to admit but it's the truth. Taking a risk is what a fighter is all about, scared of course. Apprehending it, controlling it. Realizing 99 percent of all fighters are feeling exactly what you're going through, believe me it's called humanity and humility.

In the dressing room before the fight, I was a little tight, stiff, and honestly scared beyond measure. If I were to think too much, that could distract and destroy me. *"Mind over matter Adam, you can do it".* I recall during my entrance to the ring, that I consciously had to come in with a front on my face to tame the panic that wanted to take control. With the Grant brothers at my side and the late Mr.

Bob Miller as my cut man, I stepped into the ring before the largest crowd of my career. *"This is it Adam, stay focused."*

The fight was scheduled for 8 rounds in front of an electric crowd of 9000. This was the perfect opportunity to showcase my skills against Alex, who was about to enter his last hurrah as there were rumors of Alex contemplating retirement. Despite the pressure, I maintained my composure, ultimately stopping him in the sixth round. Looking back, I realized I may have been an arrogant piece of shit, but I admit I was still a kid. I harbor no ill will toward Alex. In fact, I have nothing but respect and gratitude for the influence he had and the opportunity he had presented me.

Alex Hilton, I love you, even though you bullied Jeff and I in our beginnings. I believe you had your reasons.

Peace, love, and respect, always. I wish you nothing but the best. GOD BLESS AND THANK YOU!

CHAPTER 16: An Unexpected Challenge...

Now my name would be out there, all over the news, in the papers, signing autographs, and doing pretty darn good for a 25-year-old! It was possible that I was on a cloud as I would encounter a little, but good, setback in the time to come.

Following the Hilton fight, the focus shifted to reaching the 147-pound weight class. Given my height, many believed it was the right weight for me. My next fight was slated for March 3rd, 2005, with intentions to compete as a welterweight in the coming year. We agreed to a contract with a weight limit no higher than 151, a common practice for non-title fights.

Enter the world of nutrition. I was assigned a personal nutritionist by management. A move met with mixed emotions as I really enjoy the freedom eating what I want, when I want. I won't lie, I wasn't very happy. Training vigorously was one thing but restricting my food intake felt like another battle altogether. Of course I was able to eat, but I was under the impression that I would have to starve myself. Back then, I didn't have the knowledge I have today and realize now how big of a mistake that approach was. Starving oneself is a rookie mistake, leading to overindulgence later on. The trick is, ladies and gentlemen (I'm going to have to start charging now), to eat only what is required. All you need is a little something in your stomach to prevent the feeling of hunger. Savoring every bite and appreciating the nourishment it provides.

March 3rd, 2005 had arrived. My last two fights had come with their own respective pressures, but this one had less hype, and it was decided that it would be held back at the once outgrown Club Soda. Unknowingly at the time, this would be my last fight at this venue. I had respected my 151 lbs obligation at the weigh-in the day prior and my lowest to date. I literally looked like a Skeleton! Despite the physical, mental, and emotional challenges of making weight, I entered the ring against Justin Danforth from Milwaukee, USA. With the fight broadcasted on the Vox network, I felt obligated to review and learn from my performance afterwards.

I would capture the victory that night with a TKO in the 5thround. Straight up, I asked Yvon for an easier fight because my last 2 were big ones. Assuming I would be eligible for a less intense fight, I would learn later in life that I did not have the right mindset. I was looking for an easy route, but for myself I wasn't focused. There is no easy route in this profession. A true fighter does not ask for this or that, he shuts his mouth and performs no matter how he feels. It's called being a professional. This is all said by the legendary late great boxing philosopher, Mr. Cuss D'Amato.

Post-fight, an unexpected challenge emerged from Mr. Desormiers, sparking intrigue and anticipation. He would enter the ring and would openly challenge me on the mic, which was an unexpected but strategic career move on his part. I'm assuming he expected that I would capture the

Canadian Title then fight him. I thought he made a good move anyhow as really it just gets people talking about us and will make more money appear in the bout's purse just because of the added interest. This is something that can still be seen with any combative sport to this day. Lots of people are inspired by classical matchups, Stephane was the biggest attractor for selling tickets and I would be number two. With our paths seemingly converging, an exciting showdown loomed on the horizon.

CHAPTER 17: Hope on the Horizon: Battling Internal Turmoil.

My managers (Adam Harris and Paul Michaud), my girlfriend Caroline, and I reached a collective decision. It was time for me to confront my struggles with alcohol through therapy. Recognizing the need to face my demons if I wanted to have a better control of my mind.

I temporarily vanished from the boxing scene, as I grappled with internal battles involving alcohol and drugs. Listen, I was young, and I had just come off a victory over a guy I looked up to. Emotionally, I was having trouble grasping this and couldn't accept the reality of it.

Emerging from therapy, I was met with unwavering support from those around me. Their pride in my progress fueled our shared vision of vying for the Canadian welterweight title at 147 pounds. It was a stark reminder that despite our best-laid plans, life often takes unexpected turns.

Meanwhile, Adam Harris took charge of promoting my upcoming title fight against Brooke Wellby from Manitoba. Adam's promotional efforts were exceptional, organizing a bus tour with fellow fighters and trainer Howard Grant to drum up anticipation for the title fight scheduled for June 23, 2005. From bars and clubs to restaurants and events, the tour, complete with ring girls, was a testament to Adam's dedication and skill in promotion.

Wellby s'est trouvé une excuse

Adam Green devait normalement affronter Brooke Wellby pour le titre canadien des poids moyens à la fin juin, mais le boxeur de Winnipeg n'a pas réussi le test médical.

CHARLES POULIN

Une excuse qui en fait encore sourciller plusieurs, dont Green lui-même.

« Il se surnomme *Schoolboy* (écolier), moi, je dirais plutôt *Schoolgirl* ! a lancé Green. Qu'il vienne m'affronter, je vais lui donner une leçon ! »

Une reprise du combat devrait avoir lieu cet automne, mais si Wellby ne peut se battre, il est fort probable que l'Association canadienne de boxe amateur (ACBA) lui retire la ceinture et implique Green dans le combat de championnat.

Les chances seraient très grandes qu'il affronte son copain Stéphane Desormiers, qui lui aussi veut mettre la main sur la précieuse ceinture.

« Il n'y a personne avec assez de talent au Canada pour me battre », affirme sans broncher Desormiers.

Parions que Green voit les choses autrement...

The West Island Times • Friday, May 27, 2005

Boxing Tour Includes West Island

Ring Side
Continued from Front Page

Howard Grant trains MacIlroy and Green and was, along with his brother and 5th ranked in the world Otis "Magic" Grant, present for the opulent announcement.

Welterweight Stéphane Desormier will also get a fight with an undetermined opponent and should he and Green win, both will square off this fall in what many expert believe to be one of the most promising fights of the year.

In an effort to keep the buzz going, there will be a public training session June 3, 4 and 5th at John Scotti Automobile from 12 pm to 3 pm, will be held a public training for the June 18th Gala at the Bell Center, all the boxers from this Gala will be present.

During the festivities of the Canadian Grand Prix on June 9th along Crescent street , Otis Grant will be part of the F1 pit stop competition in front of more than 200 000 fans.

On a local level, the promoters will be spreading the word about the upcoming championship fight on the West Island by visiting many bars of the West Island this coming, Friday and Saturday.

Tickets are already on sale and can be purchased by calling R.F.I. Promotions at 968-8843.

Howard Grant

Adam Green

Green on fast track for title

Faces Wellby in Beaconsfield on June 23 for Canadian welterweight championship

HERB ZURKOWSKY
THE GAZETTE

He lacks experience, but not confidence.

Despite fighting only 11 times as a pro, Châteauguay's Adam Green is getting a shot at the Canadian welterweight championship. He'll meet titleholder Brooke Wellby of Winnipeg on June 23 in the 12-round main event at Club West Island in Beaconsfield. Although Wellby sports a 31-15-3 record, including 10 knockouts, Green, 24, has no doubt the belt will change hands that night.

"Nothing can get in my way. Experience won't stop me," said Green, 10-1-0 with five KOs. "It's not a question of experience. I'm going to put so much pressure on him that he'll go to the bathroom in his pants.

"You've never seen a fighter like me."

It's difficult to determine a boxer's strengths and weaknesses this early in a career. Green is a busy fighter who comes straight at his opponent, puts his head down and flails away. He beat an aging Alex Hilton, the former Canadian middleweight champ, December, stopping him in six rounds. But a month earlier, Green lost a six-round unanimous decision to Canadian aspirant Matt O'Brien, who's undefeated and on next month's undercard.

"I think I've got the better guy. I'm not concerned," said Howard Grant, Green's trainer. "I hope Adam goes in with his head straight. If he does, he'll be OK. He works hard, trains hard and doesn't cut corners. I'm not worried about his condition.

"I think he's ready. He deserves it."

It's hard to know what to expect from Wellby, 29. At 6-foot-1, he'll carry a six-inch height advantage into the ring. A reach advantage, too, presumably. He's also a southpaw, although Green is undefeated in four bouts against left-handers and has the luxury of sparring with one of the best, former World Boxing Organization champ Otis Grant.

But Wellby, who fought Darren Kenny last night for the fourth time in his career, has had trouble with his fluctuating weight. He weighed 170 – 23 pounds over the welterweight limit, two months ago, when he lost an eight-round split-decision to Verdell Smith in Green Bay.

Wellby has three defeats and a draw in his last four bouts. He won the Canadian title in November 2003, against Rico Tan.

"I like Adam's heart," trainer Grant said. "He's got a good chin and he's got balls. He's not scared to fight, get hit and hit back. I think he'd leave his soul in the ring if it came down to it."

The card's being promoted by Groupe Yvon Michel in conjunction with Real Fighting Irish, a West Island company headed by Adam Harris, son of former NHL defenceman Ron Harris.

"I'm getting my teeth cut (in promotions) and trying to bring something back," said the 30-year-old, who boxed as an amateur and has dabbled in mixed martial arts, along with Ultimate Fighting. "Boxing has always been a passion of mine. It's had a huge impact on my life."

Six preliminary bouts are on tap. Club capacity is expected to be 1,500. More than 350 tickets have been sold. For more information, telephone (514) 908-9090.

Note — Super-lightweight champ **Hermann Ngoudjo** of Montreal, who defended his title Saturday against Juan Carlos Rodriguez, has been named the North American Boxing Federation's prospect of the year.

hzurkowsky@thegazette.canwest.com

CHAPTER 18: Plot Twists and Knockouts

Unfortunately, the Canadian welterweight title against Brooke Wellby fell through since he "couldn't" make the weight (I feel like he didn't want to make the weight). This was heartbreaking as my chances of winning were considered quite high. My next opponent would instead be Frankie Sanchez, slated to be my first 10-round bout, in an aspiration to get another shot at the title.

On July 13, 2005, Frankie Sanchez, with his extensive experience against formidable opponents like David Diaz and Kermit Cintron, posed a significant challenge. However, complications arose as Frankie failed to meet the agreed-upon weight, forcing me to compromise and fight at my heaviest ever, 163.5 lbs. Despite this, I entered the ring in peak condition, visually trim and ready to make an impact. In the fifth round, the fight ended abruptly with a TKO, adding another win to my impressive record, which now stood at 11-1 (5 KO's).

That night's undercard featured an exciting turn of events in my rivalry with Stephane Desormiers. Stephane, previously undefeated in 11 fights, was showcasing good power with a streak of five 1stround KOs. He started off looking good, throwing his common combinations and in-between, he got caught with a short-left hook, that left him paralyzed on the floor for a couple of seconds. He received a taste of his own medicine by dropping in the 1stround!

The incident left everyone in a state of shock. Despite his demoralization, Stephane would later prove that this setback was merely a wake-up call for him.

CHAPTER 19: Mountain Mornings in Sin City.

In August of that year, Adam Harris arranged for me to travel to Las Vegas, where I found myself training at the world-famous Mayweather Boxing Club- I kid you not, I was actually at Floyd Mayweather's gym! It was an incredible opportunity, but looking back, I regret not having the courage to ask about meeting the great Floyd Mayweather Jr. himself. Don't get me wrong, I'm still incredibly grateful and honoured to have interacted with legends like Roger Mayweather, Floyd Mayweather Sr., Raphael Garcia, and Leonard Ellerbe during my two-week stay. My training partner was Mamadou Thiam, a renowned boxer from France. He had a stellar career and even faced off against the elite Felix Trinidad, which was a remarkable achievement since Felix had a victory over Oscar Dela Hoya, something extremely impressive to have on your boxing resume.

Our daily routine in Las Vegas was rigorous yet rewarding. Mamadou Thiam and I would start jogging at 6 am in the mountains, followed by a brief rest and breakfast in my room. Then, at 10:45 am, we headed to Mayweather's gym for an 11 am training session with the legendary Uncle Roger. Initially, Roger seemed to take a liking to me, but that changed when I sparred with Wes Ferguson, a talented yet cocky boxer, during my third session. I allowed Wes to get into my head, and Roger distanced himself from me thereafter. It was a lesson learnt the hard way: actions speak louder than words, especially in the ring.

Despite the setback with Roger, I found solace in the genuine humility and kindness of Leonard Ellerbe. He seemed to appreciate my presence, which was a comforting vibe to receive. I didn't interact much with Floyd Mayweather Sr., but I thoroughly enjoyed the company of Raphiel Garcia, Floyd's cutman, whose jokes and good humor lightened the atmosphere.

Sparring sessions with Mamadou were a highlight for me. His wealth of experience made him a smooth and enjoyable partner to work with as sparring with less experienced boxers can be unpredictable. It presented opportunities for growth and adaptation. In the later part of his career, Mamadou would be bested in a fight against my old Quebec teammate, Sebastien Demers. I think back to our time training together in Las Vegas with pride.

CHAPTER 20: The Cost of Deviation: Sticking to the Game Plan

Adam Harris was determined to secure a welterweight title fight for me. Unfortunately, Brooke Wellby was no longer in the picture, unable to make the 147-pound limit. Despite the setback, we pressed on, acknowledging that everything happens for a reason.

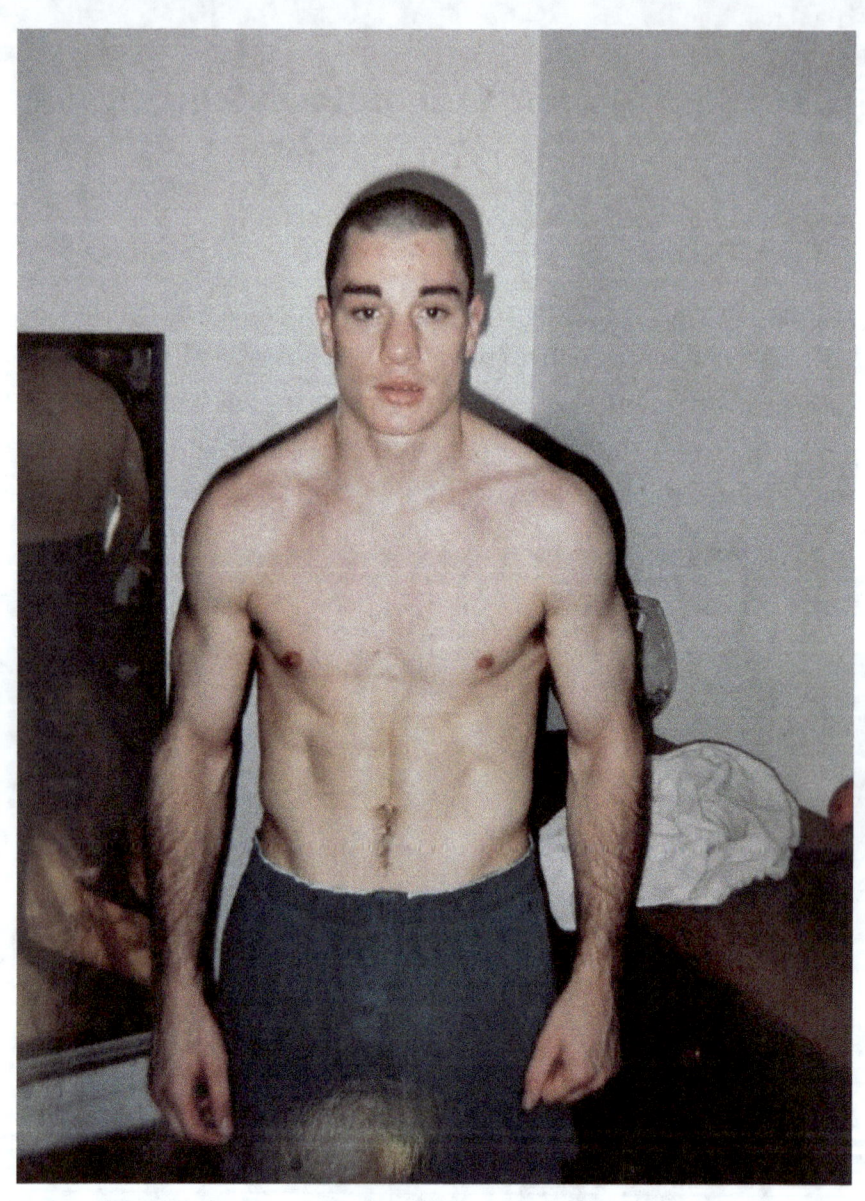

Enter Victor Lupo, my next opponent hailing from Romania but making his mark in Canada. Our showdown was set for November 3rd, 2005, with the Canadian welterweight title on the line. It was my first attempt at hitting the 147-pound mark, and I managed to make weight. However, going the full 10 rounds proved to be a challenge.

Lors d'un point de presse tenu hier à Pointe-Claire, Adam Green a promis de battre son adversaire, le Torontois d'origine roumaine, Victor Lupo, en moins de huit rounds, le 2 novembre, lors d'un match de championnat canadien des poids mi-moyens disputé au Métropolis.

Match de championnat canadien des poids mi-moyens le 2 novembre au Métropo[lis]

« Je vais gagner en moins de huit rounds »

– Adam Gre[en]

Les combats de championnats canadiens de boxe professionnelle dans la division des poids mi-moyens (147 livres) ont longtemps eu la cote sur le territoire québécois.

DANIEL
CLOUTIER
Le Journal de Montréal

Ils permettaient fréquemment de remplir le Forum et le centre Paul-Sauvé dans les années 1960, 1970 et 1980.

Le chef des opérations au sein du groupe GYM, Yvon Michel, croit qu'ils vont redevenir populaires dans les mois à venir.

« Au début des années 1970, nos principaux boxeurs dans la division des mi-moyens étaient Donato Paduano et Fernand Marcotte, tandis que les années 1980, Davey Hilton et Mario Cusson occupaient toute la place », souligne Michel.

« Lorsque ces gars s'affrontaient, les arénas étaient pleins à craquer. Nous allons pouvoir faire revivre cette ambiance dans les mois à venir avec Stéphane Désormiers, Adam Green et Victor Lupo. »

Le gagnant affronterait Désormiers

Hier après-midi, dans le cadre d'une conférence de presse tenue au Pub McKibbins de Pointe-Claire, le groupe GYM a confirmé la tenue d'un match de championnat canadien des 147 livres entre le Torontois d'origine roumaine Victor Lupo et le Québécois Adam Green.

Cet affrontement de 10 rounds sera disputé le 2 novembre au Métropolis, dans le cadre d'un BoxeRock.

Tout indique que le vainqueur fera face à Désormiers, un boxeur de Terrebonne, au début 2006.

« Je rêve depuis bien des années de me faire appeler le Champ, et ça va enfin [se] matérialiser le 2 novembre, a expli[qué] Green, un boxeur d'Ormstown. Je v[ais] gagner ce combat-là, je vous l'assure.

« Lupo se bat comme un enragé, m[ais] je boxe intelligemment. Un boxe[ur] indiscipliné comme Lupo ne viendra [pas] à bout d'un boxeur aussi intelli[gent] et méthodique que moi. Il commet t[rop] d'erreurs. Je vous prédis que je v[ais] gagner en moins de huit rounds. »

Lupo (9-0-0) a souri en entendant [les] propos de Green (11-1-0).

« Le titre canadien n'est qu'une é[tape] pour moi. C'est le titre mondial qu[e je] vise, a déclaré le Torontois. Mais co[mme] je vis maintenant en permanen[ce à] Toronto, c'est normal que le ti[tre] canadien me tienne à cœur. Ceux [qui] disent que je déteste Green à m[e le] confesser font erreur.

« Je n'ai rien contre lui. Toutefois, [il est] dans mon chemin, et je me chargera[i de] l'enlever de là. Si Green croit pouvo[ir] battre le 2 novembre, il rêve en coule[ur. »]

I started strong, winning the first three out of four rounds. Reflecting on the fight, I realized that maintaining mental focus for such a long battle was a formidable task, especially for a young boxer like myself. Lupo's relentless pressure of throwing non-stop punches exposed a critical flaw in my approach. By allowing him to enter my bubble, I lost sight of myself, a costly mistake in the ring. As fatigue set in, my focus waned. Going the distance, especially with the Canadian title at stake, proved to be mentally taxing. In the end, I suffered my second defeat as a professional, losing by decision.

It's no secret that fatigue is inevitable in boxing. The key lies in smart decision-making, particularly in managing thoughts during crucial moments. I learned that leveraging my boxing skills would have been more effective than engaging in a battle of slugging. Fighting smarter and not harder is easier said than done, but the results are worth pursuing.

In hindsight, I recognized that my attempt to wear down Lupo was misguided. Instead of playing to my strengths, I deviated from my game plan. It was a valuable teaching moment, reinforcing the importance of maintaining focus and strategic thinking inside that ring. *"Bad move Adam, lesson learnt"*.

CHAPTER 21: Taste of Victory: Sweet Success.

When I first embarked on my journey as a professional boxer, the title of champion seemed like a distant dream. However, after some reflection following my last fight, my goals became clearer. No more fighting at 147 for me; it was a drain on my energy reserves. My focus shifted towards becoming a champion in the sport of boxing.

On February 2, 2006, I faced a different challenge in Claudio Ortiz. While he may have lacked skill, he made up for it with raw toughness. Manitoban born Ortiz brought his own flair to the ring. Our bout was for the Super Welterweight Quebec Title, adding an extra layer of significance. Some may have seen it as an intriguing matchup, given Ortiz's showmanship. However, I remained focused on the task at hand.

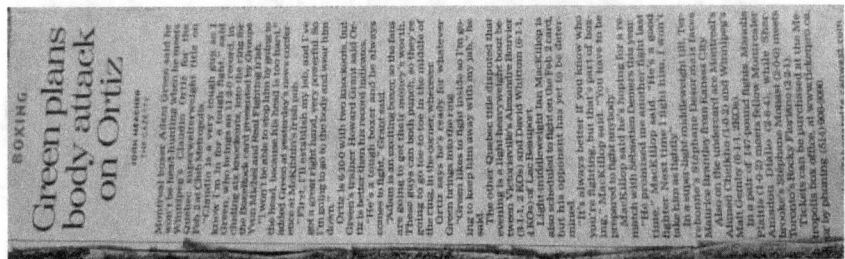

That night, I achieved my first major milestone by becoming the Champion of Quebec. It was a moment of triumph, not just for me but also for Desormiers, who found redemption on the undercard with an eight-round unanimous decision victory.

I dedicate this victory to my beloved mother, whose culinary talents inspired me both inside and outside the ring. Her delicious creations, like salmon with sweet potatoes and kale, fueled my body and mind for success. Today, as I meticulously plan my meals a week in advance for optimal performance, I carry her legacy with me.

Desormiers next opponent for boxer Green

Chateauguay boxer Adam Green continues his comeback trail tonight when he takes on highly-rated Stéphane Desormiers at Club Metropole in Montreal.

DAN ROSENBURG

Adam Green (Photo archives)

Back in November, Green became a victim of his own folly when he was accused of showboating and losing concentration in a defeat suffered at the hands of Victor Lupo.

Green learned his lesson, apparently. In his last fight he redeemed himself by winning the Quebec super-welterweight title at Montreal's Club Metropolis, going the eight-round distance for the first time in his career. Green outpointed Claudio Ortiz of Manitoba by a unanimous decision to bolster his record to an impressive 12-2.

"I stayed focused the whole fight, even when he (Ortiz) started clowning around," Green told reporters afterwards. "As far as I'm concerned, I dominated the fight. I have a much cleaner style than he does. He tried to throw big, looping rights. But he never hurt me once all fight." Ortiz was even penalized two points for illegal blows.

Green is now targeting the Canadian super-middleweight crown held by Sébastien Demers.

"The Quebec title is only a stepping stone for me," said the Green Machine. "I want to go much further than that. The next step will be the 154-pound Canadian championship. I am very energetic at that weight."

Green, 25, has been boxing for 11 years. The grandson of author and former Billings and Kahnawake Survival School teacher H. Gordon Green, Adam moved to Chateauguay from Ormstown last year.

Although Green fights for Groupe Yvon Michel in conjunction with the Real Fighting Irish organization headed up by promoter Adam Harris, the boxer finds humor in the fact that he is not Irish.

"I've got more Danish and Italian blood in me than Irish," he quipped.

Stéphane Désormiers : « Ce sera une bataille féroce »

Il affrontera Adam Green pour la ceinture québécoise des 154 livres, mercredi soir au Métropolis

DANIEL CLOUTIER

Dans le milieu de la boxe professionnelle locale, on souhaitait ardemment voir se concrétiser un affrontement entre deux longtemps pugilistes associés au groupe GYM, Adam Green et Stéphane Désormiers. Ce combat se matérialisera mercredi soir au Métropolis.

Green (12-2-0), un boxeur de Châteauguay, risquera alors sa ceinture québécoise des super-mi-moyens (154 livres).

Les partisans, ceux de Green et une foule d'amateurs de boxe du Québec, souhaitaient ça depuis fort longtemps et, enfin, ça va se concrétiser, a indiqué Désormiers bien. Ce sera une bataille féroce, aucun doute là-dessus. Nous avons tous les deux un tempérament fougueux. »

Désormiers (15-1-0), un pugiliste de Terrebonne, avoue qu'il s'attend à être impliqué dans le combat le plus spectaculaire de sa carrière.

« Je n'aurai aucun répit dans ce combat, a-t-il admis. Green est tenace sans bon sens, et il est salaud chaque fois que l'adversaire le frustre. Il ne se gêne pas pour forcer tête basse.

« Je m'attends effectivement que soit un affrontement extrêmement âpre, mais j'ai la conviction que je vais apprécier l'expérience. J'adore les combats disputés sous haute tension. Plus je suis nerveux, plus je suis énergique et performant.

« De plus, mon dernier combat, qui m'a opposé à l'Américain Maurice Brantley (25-12-0), m'a grandement aidé à me préparer pour cet affrontement avec Green. C'était un match très rude. »

À la limite

« Cette fois, nous devrions logiquement atteindre la limite des 10 rounds, mais si l'un de nous deux croule dans le ring à un moment ou à un autre, ce sera certainement lui, a affirmé Désormiers. Green cogne dur, mais ses coups ne sont pas assez rapides pour m'envoyer au tapis. »

« S'il détrône Green à titre de champion du Québec, Désormiers lancera un défi au champion mondial des poids mi-moyens (147 livres), le Torontois d'origine roumaine Victor Lupo.

« Green et moi allons nous affronter à un poids de 158 ou 154 livres mercredi, mais lorsque chez les 147 livres et tout a fait naturel pour moi, a souligné Désormiers. Alors, je vais d'abord régler son compte à Green, puis lancer un défi à Lupo. »

CHAPTER 22: Friends Turned Foes: Clash of the Titans.

This was it, the moment that defined my career, the culmination of years of training and dedication. The fight everyone had been waiting for: Adam Green versus Stephane Desormiers. He wasn't just my opponent; he was my training partner, my teammate, and my friend. Stephane had a significant following, especially from our gym. We had spared countless times, knowing each other's strengths and weaknesses inside and out. It was inevitable that we would eventually face off in the ring.

Stephane hailed from Terrebonne, where he would eventually open his own gym that continues to this day. We shared the same trainers, the same gym, and the same promoters. However, for this fight, we had to have separate training schedules and each choosing our own trainers for the last three weeks. I trained with Marc Seyer, while Stephane opted for Marc Ramsey, a renowned trainer in Canada.

The fight was scheduled for April 13, 2006, for the Jr. Middleweight Quebec Title. In the weeks leading up to the bout, my manager arranged for me to train in St. Hyacinthe with Marc Seyer and Sebas Demers. The sparring sessions were intense, preparing me for the challenge ahead.

There would be a minor setback as for some reason the fight would be postponed for 2 weeks. The date would be

April 26th, 2006. Stephane took this setback in a good way, saying it gave him more time to get in even better condition. Where I approached it in the sense that I'm ready now. It's all about peaking at the right time. That's exactly where your experience and sense of your own body takes place. I was young and dumb, and I should have had the same mentality as Stephane and get myself in even better shape. I was eager to step into the ring.

This was the moment of truth; my mind was a racehorse. I remember warming up in my dressing room, when my father entered the room and shook his head and said "it's your night". He thought I had a good aura around me, and he was right. I might have lost the first round, but after that I would be dominating all the rounds up until the 9th. The most important aspect in boxing is what is going on inside your mind during the heat of battle, when you're at your end limits and getting hurt. That's when it's crucial to have positive thoughts. No matter what scenario occurs, you always must find a way to have faith in your skills and self to capture the victory. That's what you can call a champion!

Something I learned later in life and allows me to live in peace today is the belief that "everything happens for a reason". Going into this fight, the crowd would not be my largest, but it was by far the most intense, passionate, and on edge crowd that I ever had the honor of entertaining. At the age of 25, I made my ring entrance as the Québec Junior Middleweight Champion for my first title defense. I would be in a mental bubble that would work most of the night, but when we did our face-to-face before the fight, I was full of intense emotions. As I was looking at Stephane straight in the eyes, I was saying to myself "*wtf is going on here*" as I was looking at Stephane straight in the eyes.

Shit! This is my training partner, my friend and now my rival. Usually when we spared, I felt I could keep the tempo with my jab alone, but not tonight. He would be in tip-top condition, and so was I. We would both have our advantages and disadvantages. My advantage would be the fact that I had already been 10 rounds against Victor Lupo. I thought we both had nice styles to watch (signature styles make fights) and our techniques would complement one another. This would go down as fight of the year in 2006.

Before I get to the results, this would be the fight that kept me hungry after all these years. Bottom line, I would be going in the 10th round ahead on all the scorecards (87-83, 86-84 x2). This is when the trainer should get some credit for his last word in-between the 9th and 10th round. By God! You can hear Marc Ramsey tell Stephane on the video "DON'T LEAVE REGRET IN THE RING! LAST ROUND! DO IT FOR YOUR KIDS, IF YOU CAN'T DO IT FOR YOURSELF!" Best example of a wakeup call.

My strategy was to keep him at the end of my jab. Knowing he was behind, he threw a haymaker that caught me, and I would be in big trouble. He was aware and pounced on his opportunity. It paid off for Stephane as I grabbed a hold of him thinking *"if I'm going down, you are coming with me"*. Gerry Bolen, the referee, was aware that I got hit before Stephane and I went down. When we arose, Gerry caught me off guard with a standing 8. He asked me "can you continue" and I confirmed. In for the kill, Stephane would continue to hunt for the KO. It all went by so fast that I prioritized defense over offense which ultimately cost me the fight. That was my biggest regret; not having balls to retaliate. It took me a long time to forgive myself. *"Everything happens for a reason"* and Gerry would end up stopping the fight. That was it. The title was lost.

At the point in the 8thround where we both fell to the floor; you could tell we were struggling. It would take everything to stand back up on our feet which highlights the theme of my story: "power of the mind". The complex sum of your actions which can be displayed in a fraction of a second. It's all an experience, and you will have to face it in a real situation to literally comprehend what I'm saying.

There would be a brawl in the crowd afterwards, and I heard that my father allegedly threw his beer at Gerry. I always like to put on a good show for the crowd and get them on the edge of their seat, but it's a better feeling when the victory comes with it. Listen, I was not good, and I was pretty much ready to say goodbye to boxing forever. That was just the beginning as I would encounter a couple more setbacks.

I always find it fascinating, when everyone believes you have no chance in hell and defies the odds by obtaining the upset. That's exactly what Stephane would achieve that night. What I should have done was grab hold of him and not let go. Even if the ref would call break, hold on for dear life until my head would clear, and I could catch my breath.

That would be my lesson of the night. Good job champ you were the better man that night, nothing else that I could say. I was 25 years old, and I didn't take it at all in a good way.

I've seen on numerous occasions, boxers taking a beating, and even getting knocked down multiple times in a round; Diego Corrales vs Juan Castillo and George Foreman vs Ron Lyle are fights that come to mind. The other lesson I learnt was how I opened my big mouth and said in the *Journal de Montreal that* "Stephane won't last until the 10th round". Well that came right back in my face with a hard smack!

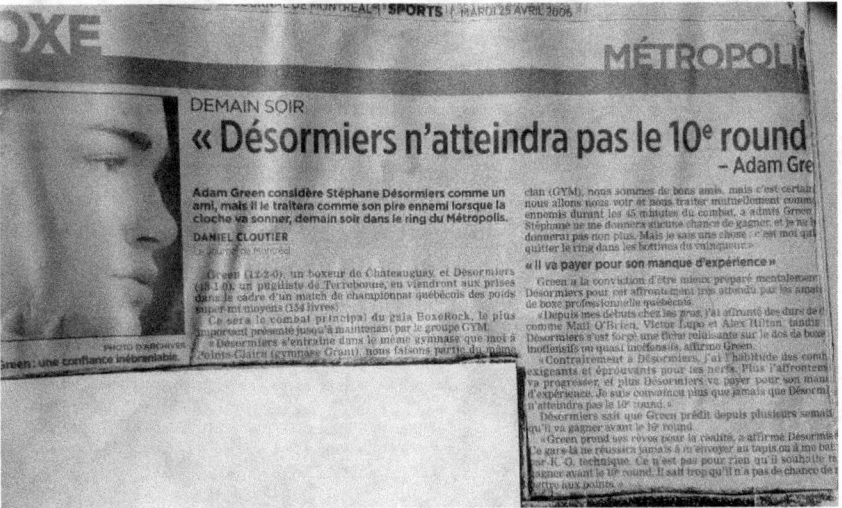

Damn, what a battle!

Now take this as a lesson young fighters, when the time comes inside the ring, stay confident, humble, show respect, and be proud of your actions, not your words.

Back to the drawing board and everyone would conclude they wanted to see a rematch.

Désormiers comeback TKOs Chateauguay boxer
Ormstown

Adam Green (Photo archives)

Prior to their Quebec super-welterweight (154-pound) title match at the Metropolis in Montreal last Wednesday, defending champion Adam Green of Chateauguay went on record as saying that his tenacity would wear down the resistance and morale of opponent Stéphane Désormiers of Terrebonne. According to those who attended the match, the opposite took place.

DAN ROSENBURG

From all reports, Désormiers was 'way behind on points after nine rounds of their 10-round bout. But Désormiers gave it his all in the final round to stop Green on a technical knockout.

The dramatic come-from-behind victory boosted Désormiers' ledger to 14-1, while Green's record slipped to 12-3.

Green had won his last previous fight on points over Claudio Ortiz of Manitoba, going the eight-round distance for the first time in his professional career.

Green, who calls himself "The Green Machine", is the grandson of the late H. Gordon Green, a former teacher at Howard S. Billings Regional High School and the Kahnawake Survival School.

In another battle of note on the card, Hercules Kyvelos (24-2) of Laval returned to a Montreal ring for the first time in five years and knocked out Jeff Carpenter of the U.S. midway through the second round.

CHAPTER 23: The Swing Bout Saga: Waiting in Limbo

The plan was clear: both of us would have a tune-up fight before the rematch. That was the goal and the next step in my journey. Scheduled for June 23rd, 2006, at the Uniprix Stadium in Montreal, my opponent was initially from Costa Rica, typically signaling a favorable matchup.

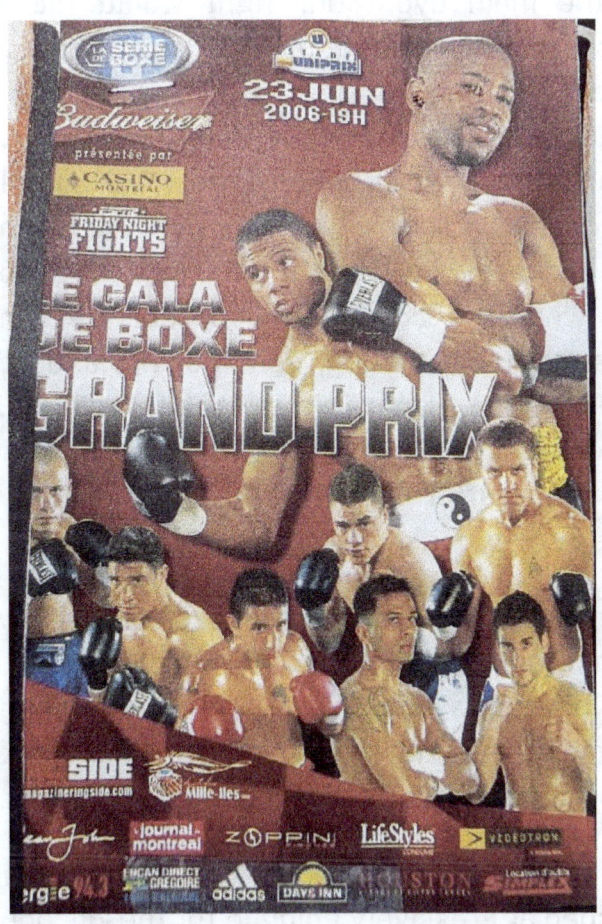

However, the last-minute change brought Stephan Boyd, a 6'2" fighter from Toronto, into the ring. I had heard of him since my sparring partner Walid Smichet had fought him on the undercard of my O'Brien fight in 2004. Boyd had been out boxing him for 3 quarters of the fight, but Walid came back with a last round knockout. It was a thriller! This must have been one exciting night for the crowd.

Our fight was the "swing bout," meaning its timing depended on the pace of the previous fights. If there was an early knock-out that would create a gap in the schedule before the main event our fight would fill that gap otherwise it would be put at the very end of the night. I was on stand-by in my dressing room since 6:30 pm being prompted multiple times "start warming up, you're next," only to be told to wait after some time. The mental toll and frustration this had on me was intense. They say the actual fight is the easy part about boxing, so you can only imagine what the combination of countless hours of relentless training, dieting, conditioning, and now false starts has on a person. This is all part of being a professional boxer. Finally, I found myself entering the ring sometime after midnight, after the main event had concluded and much of the crowd had dispersed.

Boyd dominated the early rounds, peppering me with jabs, right hands, uppercuts, and hooks. My face took a beating, swelling and threatening to close shut. After the second round, my trainer, Howard Grant, issued a warning: if I didn't show improvement, he would stop the fight.

In the third round, I managed to land a good combination and pursued aggressively going in for the kill, only for the stadium lights to suddenly go out. It was a bizarre interruption, providing Boyd with a brief window of recovery. When the lights returned, he resumed his assault, prompting Howard to throw in the towel, signaling the end of the fight. What can I say, it wasn't meant to be. Defeated and discouraged, I contemplated leaving boxing behind for good. A break was much needed.

PART 3:

I would take my mind off boxing as my intention was to find a stable job, and so I'd be working full-time at the Sainte-Anne-de-Bellevue Hospital as a groundskeeper. My tasks were cutting grass, weed whacking, and collecting the garbage. This would take place for a little less than a year. I'll never forget the day I came home after work and Caroline told me she had a surprise for me, "I'm pregnant!". I had a big smile on my face and was ecstatic. We spent the rest of the day being extremely happy and holding each other. *"Now I have something to fight for"* I thought. Later my boss would give me some time off as I would prepare for my biggest fight to come.

CHAPTER 24: A Fight for Fame and Fortune: The Dave Hilton Jr. Showdown.

I would take my mind off boxing as my intention was to find a stable job, and so I'd be working full-time at the Sainte-Anne-de-Bellevue Hospital as a groundskeeper. My tasks were cutting grass, weed whacking, and collecting the garbage. This would take place for a little less than a year. I'll never forget the day I came home after work and Caroline told me she had a surprise for me, "I'm pregnant!". I had a big smile on my face and was ecstatic. We spent the rest of the day being extremely happy and holding each other. *"Now I have something to fight for"* I thought. Later my boss would give me some time off as I would prepare for my biggest fight to come.

At the beginning of 2007 Davey Hilton Jr was released from prison, with his intention to get back in the ring. Since I beat his brother Alex Hilton, Davey was looking for revenge. Their father, Dave Sr, was also looking for payback as he had his own opinion of me after having trained at their gym for so long. He thought I would be the ideal opponent for his son, a former world champion. This would be made into a reality May 1st, 2007: DAVEY HILTON JR vs ADAM GREEN at the Maurice Richard arena in Montreal.

Going back in time to 2001, Davey was going through legal battles, and I would visit him at the courthouse to truly meet for the first time. When I arrived the cameras would be stuck to me like glue wondering who I was, as some would be thinking that I was their 6th brother. We had met before but only in passing at the gym that the Hiltons trained at so this would be the first time we were able to sit down and have a conversation. I would see Davey Jr on a couple of occasions in the past, however he would always be busy boxing. Listen, the Hiltons brought me into this sport and helped build my name from the beginning. I cannot ignore the effort and work they put into me; they will always have my respect for changing my life for the better.

That would be the last time I would see Davey Jr until our press conference on April 1st, 2007.

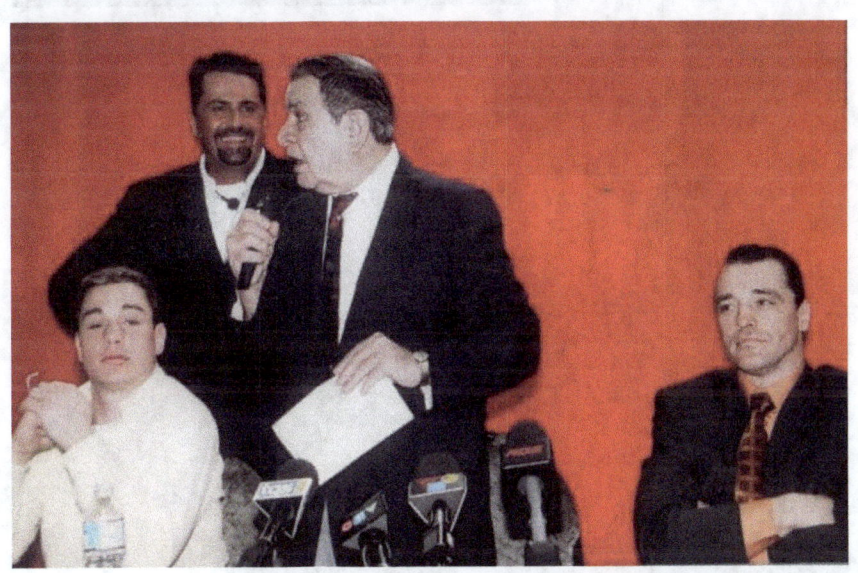

Now I have been through multiple press conferences, and there would be no more than one cameraman, but this time there would be around 7 or 8 camaras. This was big news, and I was to get my highest purse at $25 000 while Davey Jr would receive $30 000. The promoter would be the Legendary Regis Levesque, the one who promoted my fight against Alex Hilton on December 17th, 2004.

BOXE

Green libéré par le groupe GYM

Parce qu'il veut affronter Davey Hilton

Adam Green et le groupe GYM ont mis un terme définitif à leur association. Le boxeur de Châteauguay, qui s'est engagé à affronter Davey Hilton, en dépit des objections des dirigeants du groupe GYM, a tout bonnement été libéré hier matin.

DANIEL
CLOUTIER
Le Journal de Montréal

Le promoteur Régis Lévesque est celui qui a convaincu Green (12-4-0) d'accepter un affrontement avec l'aîné des *Fighting Hiltons*, qui tentera un retour à la compétition le 21 ou le 30 avril.

« Adam savait que nous n'étions aucunement intéressés à nous impliquer directement ou indirectement dans le combat que lui a proposé Régis Lévesque, mais lui, il tenait à cet affrontement », mentionnait hier Yvon Michel, le chef d'exploitation au sein du groupe GYM.

« Par conséquent, nous avons simplement décidé d'un commun accord de mettre fin à notre entente contractuelle. Nous souhaitons la meilleure chance possible à Adam, qui nous a procuré de belles émotions lors des combats qu'il a livrés sous notre gouverne. »

Âgé de 43 ans, Davey Hilton (40-2-2) a passé cinq ans derrière les barreaux pour des agressions sexuelles à répétition commises à l'égard de ses propres filles.

■ Adam Green tient à affronter Davey Hilton, ce qui ne cadre pas avec les plans du groupe GYM, qui a décidé de libérer de ses obligations.

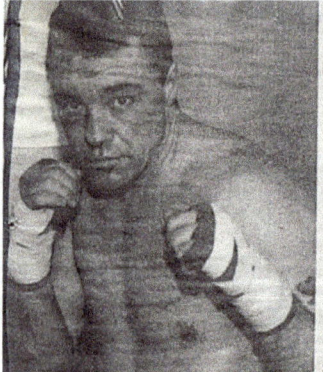

BOXE
MARDI, 1er MAI 2007
ARENA MAURICE RICHARD
FINALE 10 RDS.

DAVE HILTON
43 ANS, 157LBS, 44 COMBATS, 40-2-2
VS
ADAM GREEN
26 ANS, 157LBS, 16 COMBATS, 12-4-0

DAVE HILTON - BOURSE $30 000
ADAM GREEN - BOURSE $25 000

MARTIN BERTHIAUME
SOREL, 17 COMBATS 14-1-2
VS
PAUL CLAVET
BROSSARD, 11 COMBATS 9-1-1

4 AUTRES COMBATS À 19H30

BILLETS DISPONIBLES VIA ADMISSION
AU 514-790-1245
EN RÉGION: 1 800 361-4595
OU VIA LE WWW.ADMISSION.COM

CLUB DE BOXE CHAMPION
3270, Bélanger Est
Georges Cherry Prop.
514-376-098
514-376-4455

PRIX ADMISSION
40$, 60$, 100$, 150$, 200$
PROMOTEUR
RÉGIS LÉVESQUE

Just a few days after the press conference, on April 7th, my first child, Jakob Adam Green came into the world. I was watching my son being born and holding him in my arms for the first time. I would be a proud young father at the age of 26.

I would return with my coach Paul Roy for this fight as I always felt him, and I were an efficient team. Seeing as this fight was with a different promoter, I would have to cancel my contract with GYM and with my manager Paul Michaud. My mind was made up and I wasn't willing to walk away from the highest paid fight with the most publicity I have ever been offered. 25G's isn't something you just walk away from.

I don't recall how Steve Frishman and I met, but when we did, he played a big role in my training. Not only was he my manager but he also was my conditioning coach, where he would put me in peak condition. Probably the best condition I had been in! What is most important would be what's going on in my head. I won't lie I was intimidated by Davey; I did my best not to show it, and honestly if you're scared and unsure you're not at your best. Point final, Davey had a reputation of being a knockout artist.

Caroline and I would be aware of my mental struggles. She would reassure me by saying "He's a human being just like everyone else". Sure, he's human but he was born and raised to do this sport.

My luck would turn sour and one day, on my way to training for this fight, I was pulled over by the police and came to learn I had an unpaid ticket. This happened just before the Easter weekend and therefore the court was out until after the holiday. I would go directly to jail for the first time in my life. I was taken to Rivière-des-Prairie (RDP) Institution in Montreal. Due to the long weekend, I'd find myself remaining in custody for 5 days until court was back in session. This was a lot of unnecessary stress just before the biggest fight of my career. Lots of mixed emotions here, it was indeed messed up and very stressful. What can you do, that's what happened?

I took it well as I recall being inside with the only guy to shoot a cop and get away with it; Basil Parasiris. All because the cops had failed to enter his home legally, I believe. Other than that, I managed to stay focused as I would do my training, running, and shadow boxing. I recall there would be this cool Jewish kid that would bring me kosher food which was better than the regular meals. When the people would read the Journal de Montreal in the morning, there would be Basil on the front page and Davey and I in the sports section.

People liked us basically because we were polite, and we showed respect to one another. They loved having us there and I appreciated their comfort, especially since I was under a lot of pressure. A little love and respect are always welcomed, during these kinds of circumstances. Later I would be transferred to the Salaberry-de-Valleyfield jail for a night before going to court on Tuesday and I would be released with a fine.

I did my homework for this fight. I had good sparring with Adrian Diaconu for power, Benoit Gaudet for speed, and my third partner would be the late David Whittom, at the Claude Robillard arena. I did reach 10 rounds of sparring on 2 occasions. I was in phenomenal shape physically, the best I've ever been in.

Straight up talk now, I did it for the money and publicity. The only way you can ever ascend in this sport is to fight big names and Davey Hilton's was indeed the biggest in my realm. Unfortunately looking back, I didn't have the killer instinct for this fight, that's always a substantial necessity for any combat sport.

My home gym would be back at my old stomping ground in LaSalle. This was a fight where I didn't have to worry about money, as every Friday Paul would take me to go see Regis Levesque at his recognizable restaurant, Regis Steakhouse. He would supply me with $500, which was a reasonable advance back then. In total I would receive $5000 in advances during my training, the other $20 000 I'd get after my fight. Usually, boxers only get paid after the fight, another reason that makes this sport challenging.

I would visit my grandpa Jim, to go to my favorite spot to test my cardio at the Mount Royal's "the stairs that never end". When I got to the top, I always made sure that I kept working; shadow boxing with the mind frame *"rest'n fight"*. My grandfather didn't like the idea that I chose to become a boxer. I had heard a rumor, however, that he attended this fight, but he never told me. I will commend myself for attempting to dethrone one of Canada's top knock-out artists of all time. I did a lot of reflection for this fight. My goal was to outpoint him with sharp combinations. If you really want to beat a legend you must make it a decisive victory, there can't be any doubt. Period.

May 1st, 2007, and oh my god $20 000 payday coming my way! Bear with me now, I'm fighting the guy that I used to watch boxing all day long. He is indeed a piece of art inside that ring.

Davey would get the victory in this fight. Personally, I achieved success by overcoming adversity in the 9thround. Davey had me in trouble but the lesson I learnt fighting Stephane Desormiers of not surrendering when the fight gets tough paid off and the mistake wasn't repeated. I managed to fight my way out of it and I'm proud of that accomplishment. Being exhausted is one aspect but then getting dinged with a couple of hard shots is a whole other battle. Luckily for me, being able to withstand this assault is something I can handle better than others.

Now it was time to turn my back on boxing as everything I had visualized at the young age of 15 had come true. I was even able to go a little further by attaining the Junior Middleweight Quebec Title as well as fighting two of the Hilton brothers, boxers I had always looked up to. I figured I'm just a boy from or MS town Quebec and felt I had done enough for the time being. My motivation had literally disappeared, as my head was saying *"I just want to live a normal life"*. No more pressure, no more bullshit dieting. I want to be free. Especially now that I had my son Jake and at the time I needed a long break. Time to be a father!

CHAPTER 25: Taking a Chance: A Bold Move at the Store Counter.

I would continue to work at the Sainte-Anne-de-Bellevue Hospital for some time. My next job would be in the roofing industry. I don't recall how this happened, but my boss's name was Mr. Drinkwater. I met two men that would eventually become my good friends. Dave was high class with rich parents and Mike was a laid-back kind of guy. When we had time off, we would play hockey. I was living in Dorval, so I was grateful to have these boys as my friends.

Dave and I would share the passion of cooking, he would introduce me to one of my favorite dishes to this day, Italian sausages with sundried tomatoes and pickles.

I worked for Drinkwater for the next year, who by the end we were calling him Dinkwater. I would be communicating with my old friend Billy as he was also roofing. He was from my neck of the woods, playing hockey together and even competing in badminton doubles. I recall making it to the finals and playing in a small-town rivalry, Ormstown vs Huntingdon. We would get the victory and his reaction was to smash his racket on the floor. What a character!

I started to work for Billy who had his own successful roofing company. He was good to me and provided lots of hours. I always kind of looked up to him as I believed he was a fly kind of guy. Most of his work would be in the

West Island of Montreal and close to where I was living at the time.

Eventually Caroline and I would come across some differences, taking a break to repair the relationship. We would try to work things out and reunite, but it wouldn't last. We were together from 2002 to 2010. I was hurt and I would have to move back home with my parents.

This was one of the darkest periods of my life, I even had ideas about ending my existence. I was 31, which I consider a relatively young age. I always remember one day I would take a walk with my son, just before Caroline and I would end. We would walk to the water to find a sandy beach where we gathered up twigs and wood to start a fire. This is a memory that will always be imprinted in my mind and become a light during the darkest of hours. Jake told me he remembers, making it even more special in my heart and soul. I LOVE YOU JAKOB!

I would move back to my old room at my parents'. It was difficult for me at the time, and I felt quite lost. I recall Jake would come visit me one weekend, we were both torn up about our new reality. There was one time when he started to cry and me as well. This was in the middle of the night when the weight of such things is at their heaviest. We would fall back asleep holding each other tight. Life can be sad sometimes, between a father and son. This will be something I'll never forget.

Being back in my hometown again, I would at least have my people surrounding me. I started to work for my father, who is a successful contractor specializing in window and door installations as well as exterior finishing. I would work with him for a couple of months until my friend Bobby would have some work for me. He would focus on interior finishing inside a house, from gyprock to flooring and everything in between. Bobby secured a big contract in St-Hyacinthe, where we would pretty much live there for the duration of the work. I would meet a girl down there that seemed to really like me. She would come visit me every weekend and was a good girl with a big heart. Her name was Valerie. The relationship lasted 1 year and even though she was indeed a very genuine girl, she was just not the one for me. Bobby and I would have difficulty communicating and so working for him would come to an end. I went back to work with my father and brother, which

I'm very grateful for and feel blessed to have had the option to do so.

I am extremely thankful for the family I have been granted in life. My beloved mother would make our lunches every day, she was the best! I LOVE YOU MOM! When Jake would come to visit us every weekend, my mother would remind me how she used to take care of us, when Josh and I were growing up. Second to none for hospitality and security. Jakob loved my mother, and I don't blame him. Her name was Lynn, and she was my grandpa Jim's daughter. When she liked you, it would show with extremity? When she didn't like you... well you would get the message in a heartbeat. She could tap into a fire that can still be seen in my brother and I today. When it came to feeding the ones she loved, she was a master. I was privileged to have her as my mother and they say I look like her; my eyes and facial expressions, my demeanor and attitude. That still makes me smile to this day.

The year was 2011 and I was living with my friend Danny Pitre, who I had met while we both were working for Bobby. I had an opportunity to go work out West with all my high school friends. They were there because they followed our old classmate, Findley, making the big bucks on the oil rigs. I was lucky to have work when I got there, at the Savanna shop, while I waited for an opportunity to go and work on a rig. With a little time, I would get my chance and be proud to have been through a tough job with 12-hour shifts while making some good coin at the same time. The work schedule was 2 weeks on with 2 weeks off which I'd use to travel home to see my boy Jake while I was still staying with Danny. My mother would help me put away some money from out West, that I was able to keep up into 2022.ml would use some of it, on regaining my license back after 7 and a half years. I was lucky to have my friends which I would like to thank right here: FINDLEY MCFARLENE and ANDREW DUHEME. THANK YOU AND MAY GOD BLESS YOU ALL. I didn't get to make it out for the next season, but it didn't matter, I was blessed. I would continue to work for my father and brother.

My dad would get some of his supplies and equipment for work at a little store in town called R.S. D'Amour & Fils. Behind the counter would be this lovely little woman named Tiffany. It would start off with us talking at the store and she mentioned that she and her boyfriend weren't getting along, so like a hungry lion I would take a mental note for now. After a night with my friends, I would seem to have enough courage the next day to attempt to ask Tiffany out on a date. I walked into the store while she was working the counter, said hi and asked her for a pen and paper. Then I wrote my number and said call me sometime if you want and walked out.

CHAPTER 26: Flicker of the Boxing Flame.

Now perhaps it wasn't the following day, however she did call me, and our first date was on March 25th, 2012. To make things even better she had a boy named Lohan who would be just 1 year younger than my boy Jake. Seemed as if it was a match meant to be. Don't get me wrong we would go through many break ups, that would last up to 4 months that many people would have said "that's the end", only for us to come back together even stronger than before. Jakob and Lohan would be best friends for the years to come.

Our first of many places to live would be in between Howick and Ormstown. We were renting a house on route 138 and it would be considered a nightmare living there in the winter which would put us in debt due to inadequate heating. We would encounter a lot of highs and lows, but our little family was important to the both of us.

The way things unfolded was all a reason for me to realize that boxing would be my best route. Of course, I would make attempts only to encounter setbacks. When I flew to where I was born in Edmonton to make some serious money on the oil rigs once again, I was doing it on my own this time. Bottom line, the person giving the course would see that I didn't belong there and just like that I would be stranded in Edmonton in my motel with nowhere to go. In a state of panic, I made some critical calls and got talking to Billy, my former boss and good friend. Billy had a flight ticket for me from Edmonton to Montreal because he had family connections out there. Just like that, Billy, who I'm thanking once again, had come to my rescue. Praise this man who had saved my ass big time. I would return to Tiffany and our boys. I was considered a lucky man as that experience made me realize that I was even more determined to get back into the ring, as I was literally demoralized without the direction of boxing. It's events like this that must occur for me to receive hints into what direction I must follow.

We would eventually move to Ormstown on route 201 not far from my parent's house. I was lucky again to be working for my father. My parents would take us for breakfast one morning and right there I had a grand inspirational vision of making a comeback and even wrote on social media "plan on making a comeback, I'm only 32 and I still got some fight in me."

I'd been looking for my better half, the girl that I wanted to spend the rest of my life with. Now I would seem to have enough balls to withstand this sport once again. This was 2012 and 7 years since I last stepped into the ring. Now being 32 I knew I needed to take some serious actions and make changes. The most important factor was that the desire for boxing had resurfaced.

Adam Green

Adam Green
Dec 16, 2012

Miss my passion plan on making a comeback in the year 2013 u no I'm only 32 there still some fight left in me

See insights and ads | Boost again

👍 Like   💬 Comment   ➤ Send   ↗ Share

👍 Danny Pitre + 29   2 shares

Most relevant ⌄

Andy Rankin
Move to Ont, there a little Gym there with a great small time trainer !!!
12y   Love   1 ❤️

Steve King
Go for it
12y   Love   1 ❤️

Max Lee Smaill
Go for it bud!!!
12y   Love   1 ❤️

Andrew Singh Kooner
Do it up buddy
12y   Love   1 ❤️

CHAPTER 27: Return to the Roots: Training with Jimmy Hilton.

Jimmy Hilton would be in the process of creating a training camp/boxing school in London Ontario. My eyes were wide open and would sparkle in extreme interest to head in that direction. In the winter of 2014, I would get time off work to take my chance and so I took a train to London to go visit the one person who got me into this sport to begin with: Jimmy Hilton. When I got there, he received me with open arms and support. Now it would be all up to me to see what I had left in my reserve tank.

The first week, I would stay with Jimmy and his girlfriend to train at the gym in London. There I would have a training/sparring partner named Rambo who would be on the verge of turning professional himself. This marked the start of my comeback trial to see if I could still go the distance. I was there for one reason: I didn't like the way my boxing career ended and was ashamed especially of how I went out in the Desormiers fight. I felt I needed to redeem myself, so I wasn't there to mess around or play pretend. We proceeded every morning running with Rambo, then we would go to the gym around 2pm where Rambo and I would spar, and it was there that I discovered that I still had it. This would be a successful and fruitful first week in my comeback trail. I would receive flashbacks of this brutal business, even though I had been off for 7 years. I had always been a long-distance runner, keeping in somewhat good condition by running every chance I had. Using it as medicine to this day, I still consider this strategy to help keep me grounded, focused, and in control.

Jimmy wanted to take the training to the next level for week number 2. He was in business with Sherry Boom, the president of the Ontario Amateur Boxing Association and she would let us stay at her place for the week. Behind this would be one main reason, she had a young up-and-comer named Marko Szalai that I could train with. As I am writing this, Marko Szalai is the current Welterweight Canadian Champion and truly a promising boxer that could go all the way into winning a world title. I'm predicting it live as we speak that this kid is good. The best part is who he is as a person. Respectable, humble, and to me there is something special about him.

Changing subject for a second. One of the main reasons that got me intrigued into this sport was this classic scenario: picture this one boxer who is taking a beating and gets knocked down on several occasions. Somehow the tables turn and in the last round, behind on all the scorecards, he ends up knocking the other boxer out. I believe this is what people like to see anyhow. It would be quite thrilling to witness a boxing match that ends in this kind of fashion, wouldn't you agree? Everyone loves an underdog. Now watching a boxing match on tv is one thing. Being there live in the stadium in the heat of the action is a whole different story. You wouldn't quite see the importance of what I'm saying unless you have been to a live event yourself, then you will fully understand what I'm trying to explain. One day I am asking all you people out there to go and witness one. At least before you conclude your own assumptions about what boxing is all about. It's an experience to be had.

I had the perfect experience in London to help establish my tools for a possible comeback and it almost seems as if I had to go back to my roots for me to prepare for my new vision in boxing. I would like to take the time to thank my first trainer ever, Mr. Jimmy Hilton, once again. Love you my dear brother truly blessed to have come into your acquaintance.

CHAPTER 28: From Grief to Growth: Transforming Pain into Power.

When I got back home, I was told that my mother was diagnosed with cancer and was in poor condition. My father is a good man and took her to a place of harmony for loved ones that were on the verge of passing away. These are people that worked with the dying and made death a little less intimidating. Before this my mother was sick in bed and suffering all day for months and wouldn't say a word. My uncle Mickeal, my brother Josh, his girlfriend Jamie, Dad, Tiffany, and I would all travel to the hospice in the morning. That night mom would pass in the early morning hours. Just like that my mother was gone. A really scary sentiment as she was just 56, way too early to be leaving this world.

Now my mind was made up. Realizing that life can be cruel and take you away in a flash. Ready to take any move necessary to make things happen for my comeback. I was hungrier than ever and mad at the world as well. It was a challenging time. I LOVE

YOU MOM, I PRAY YOU ARE MORE THAN GOOD WHEREVER YOU ARE.

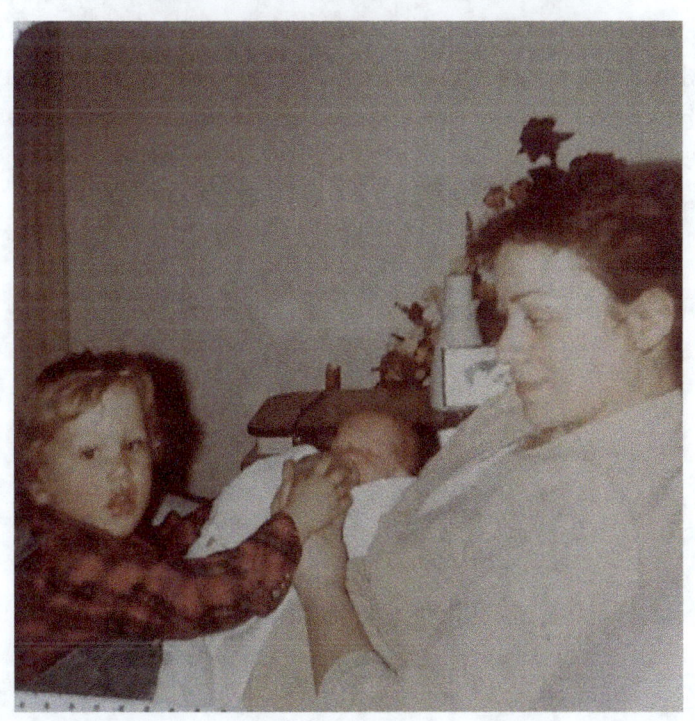

The long summer of 2014 would pass, and I would often go to Mercier for training. I would encounter the exact person I was waiting for, Daniel Lagrange. The goal was to set up an exhibition bout between him and I to help me say my goodbyes to boxing and to have closure.

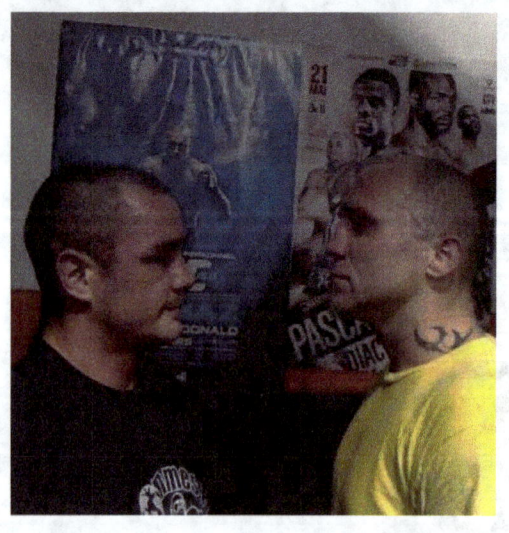

He would put these hilarious videos on Facebook that cracked me up. "GREEN, YOU BETTER BE TRAINING" the lord works in mysterious ways. The fight would never happen between us and that's when we would spar. It would be a walk in the park, but that does not diminish the fact that he has been in this sport longer than I. That means pretty much everything. Like I was trying to explain in my book. He had the knowledge which was most important and then it's been 7 and half years since I boxed. That means a lot of changes took place and he was up to date on new methods of training.

The best trick that allowed me to continue boxing was to have a small meal every 2 hours. Understanding that especially as an athlete, you should never go hungry and to tell you the truth, you sometimes lose weight because your body is always functioning. Lagrange, who was 10 years older than I, is what you call a "Gym Rat" and has seen and heard a lot of activity in the gym.

We would be in conjunction for the next 2 years every day as we were on a mission. The first step was to obtain my boxing license and all the critiques start here. The word was I was "washed up" and they were worried that I hadn't boxed for so long. Before we trained, we would always make sure our ammunition (food) was prepared with the mindset of enjoying what's in your stomach every 2 hours. That indeed would be my savior.

Dan and I had a schedule to follow, starting it all 6 days a week, 3 times a day. We started at the end of November 2014, I was on unemployment pay, that way I could make things happen faster with the little bit of income I had. Still living on route 201 with my love was perfect, it was on the way to Valleyfield where Lagrange lived as well as where the boxing gym was located.

Every day I would go pick him up. I'd get there an hour or 2 early, go into his place and discuss strictly boxing. I recall one time the topic of what song am I going to enter the ring with. In the end we both concluded it would be "The Final Countdown" by the rock band Europe. It would be a long process, day in and day out. I would be 192 lbs when I started and would drop down to 175 lbs at the end of March which would be a good weight to maintain until I would get a fight. I was smoking 5 cigarettes a day, the reason at the time I thought it would be ok, there was a world champion named Daniel Zaragoza who did exactly this. For Christ sakes if a world champion can do it then so could I, that would be my mentality.

CHAPTER 29: Defying Doubtful Critics: from Inactivity to Intensity.

"Journal de Montreal" article: *Adam Green, No Choice for the Commission but to Get Involved.*

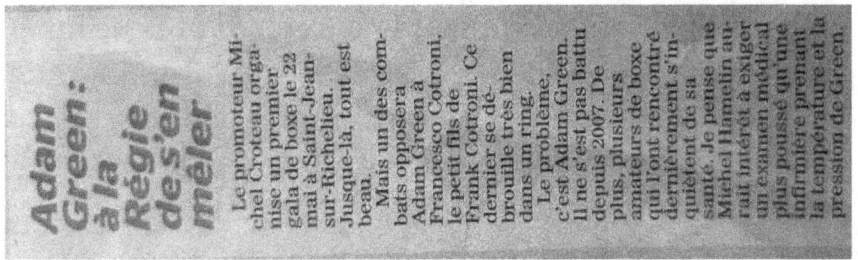

Now if I was to be straight, I took it personally in the sense that I felt insecure because I thought perhaps, they were right. *"Mind over matter Adam this is it, this is what it's always been from the get-go. A typical example of having to prove your doubters wrong."* They really couldn't believe that I was capable of fighting at all, but I knew that I wanted to at least make an attempt.

I wasn't that confident especially since I lost my last 3 fights and 8 years ago on top of things! I was 34 at this point and I knew this was it. I know myself too well and I would not be able to live the rest of my life if I didn't at least make an attempt to properly conclude my career. If I wasn't even courageous enough to do this, then the commission wouldn't be convinced that I was in proper condition to step back in the ring. They put me through numerous brain scans and Electroencephalogram (EEG) tests, it wouldn't matter as I passed every test they threw at my face. I would prove them all wrong, and their disbelief became my fire. That's what I call complete satisfaction. Now to reach top physical condition.

This is where Dan Lagrange comes into the picture and let me tell you he did a marvelous job. It had been a while since my body was looking the way it was. The name would appear, and it would be Mr. Francesco Cotroni that was to be my next opponent. On April 3rd, 2015, we had a press conference and we were on the undercard of none other than DONOVAN "RAZOR" RUDDOCK vs ERIC BARRAK! A couple of amazing heavyweight boxers and as I stated earlier in the book, I made my pro debut on Razor Ruddock's card.

Could you believe it, fighting Ruddock would be none other than my old partner in crime, Mr. Eric Barrak. I encountered Frank Cotroni for the first time when we had signed for the weight to be no heavier than 162 lbs and the fight was set for May 22nd, 2015, at the Isabelle Brasseur Stadium in Saint-Jean-Sur-Richelieu. I remember talking with Razor Rudock at the press conference that day, one of the few people that gave Mike Tyson a run for his money, twice! Along with my old sidekick in the amateur days, Mr. Eric Barrak!

This was a fight like never before. I had multiple battles, even before I was allowed to get into that ring, after this amount of time of being inactive. I had to prove myself with actions and I'm going to take the time to thank the man that brought me back after 8 years, Mr. Dan Lagrange. Without you, it wouldn't have been possible, I LOVE YOU BITCH, just as you like it. Thank you and may God bless you for eternity.

I was able to reach top condition proving to everyone and myself that I could still talk the talk and walk the walk... for now anyhow. I was lucky as Francis Lafrenière, "the People's Champ", would let me come to his gym to spar with him for my last couple of weeks for high quality sparring. Lucky for me, he would provide me with a couple of different boxers on their way up as well.

Little story behind us, he was in the amateurs and training at the Grant Brothers gym in 2004 at the same time I was training there and so we would spar together. Believe it or not he had the same style as Muhammed Ali back then! Which is completely opposite of what he does today. Now he only goes one way; forward, sticking to you like glue until you fade away. Sparring with him was an immediate realization of what this sport is all about, if I was to let my mind wander for a second, I would pay instantaneously. I'm very grateful to have had a sparring partner that not only kept my body sharp but also my mind. This was a perfect procedure to install exactly what I required from myself in order to be ready for May 22nd.

We have similar styles, as I also will stick to you and try to slowly wear you down. However, I would like to show some of the other sides of boxing as everyone is different with the way they fight. Therefore, you must be able to adapt to the different styles your opponent might bring to the table. I would like to take the time to thank "the people's champ" Mr. Francis Lafrenière, whose name is quite fitting. Congratulations on all your success! I hope you get an opportunity to pass it on to a young one with a desire as substantial as yours. Respect, you did more than well. Thank you once again.

In 2012; Lafrenière vs Cotroni! The decision went to Cotroni, having a style that gave Lafrenière trouble. That does not mean he was the better fighter just the way boxing is played out at times. They would have a rematch in 2019, and to be real, Cotroni would give Lafrenière difficulty once again. Cotroni would have an injury where Lafrenière would capitalize and stop him in round #7. Francis, I am blessed to have crossed paths with you, I truly thank you and I will never forget what you did for me. Congratulations on your career and I look forward to seeing you pass your skills on to the next generation of boxers!

CHAPTER 30: Ring Rust and Redemption: The Final Countdown.

The next step would be the weigh-in. This is where it all starts, as the boxers all meet here. This is when you show your opponent how confident you really are. It is important for me to be humble and respectful but at the same time confident, without the front. It's a fine line to walk but it's the best route for me. You could always try putting on a spectacle but then again everything will become a reality in the following 24 hours.

My lesson had been learnt and my goal was to be polite and humble, showing doubters and myself the professional I knew I could be. All business, that's where the champions are separated from the contenders. I would meet my old buddy Mr. Eric Barrack and Frank Cotroni himself. I recall he was respectful and professional, which made me feel at ease. Perhaps it wasn't the right cards for him to play. Personally, it would have been better if he had made me feel uncomfortable and made me think, just saying.

Now it would be all up to me. I felt as if I were keeping my mind at peace. I would start off by congratulating myself on all the tasks and tests that I was put through. I was beyond scared and unsure how this was going to go down. However, I had trained my ass off and it was going to be whatever was supposed to happen tomorrow night. The good news was that now I was allowed to eat! Mr. Dan had another tool to bring to the table: ice baths. A method for recuperating the body by reducing swelling and muscle damage by constricting blood vessels and decreasing metabolic activity. It also reduces strain on the cardiovascular system. Good things all around if you can handle it. What doesn't kill you, makes you stronger.

MAY 22ND 2015 VS FRANK COTRONI.

That morning had arrived and the first thing I did was go directly to Lagrange's house to spend the day with the man who helped guide me through this whole scenario. He did a great job at keeping me cool, calm, and collected. He even put a video on social media to help ease the tensions by making us all smile with his sense of humor. My buddy Jeff would join us with his brother, and we then travelled to Saint-Jean-Sur-Richelieu from there.

We did everything in our power to make things happen. I was in the right condition physically and mentally thanks to my new coach, Mr. Dan Lagrange! I know of one fighter who would achieve success after an 8-year layoff and that was George Foreman himself. He would capture the world title at the age of forty-five! I would be aiming for the Canadian Title. I used to tell everyone that I was going to win a world title, saying it, and truly believing it are two totally different paths with their own outcomes. It all starts with an image in your head. Honestly, I mentally could not reach that level, even with all the people that became world champions with the skills they had. I think I could have as well if I had more self-confidence and discipline. That is how important the power of the mind is as it plays an influential role in this sport. When I said I was going to be the Canadian Champ, I meant it. Unfortunately,

I would not be ready in 2005. However, back then I forgot to make an image in my head to manifest what I wanted. The important part they say is to picture it and then feel how you would react like it has already happened. Accepting all the sentiments that you require after you accomplished your goal and then being able to accept the reality. It just wouldn't be my time with all my setbacks, disappointments, interruptions, and apprehending life's rules. I had a lot of time to reflect on myself and what I wanted to become as a professional prize fighter.

Emotions were running high. This is where it would all come down *"Right here. OMFG!! GET A HOLD OF YOURSELF ADAM THIS IS IT."* This was a sentiment that I had turned my back on for the last 8 years. My son Jakob, family and friends were in attendance to support. This was also Tiffany and Jakob's first live event of mine. Before this fight, I had a total of 17 pro fights and 37 amateur fights which could be considered intermediate experience. This would be the moment where all my knowledge comes into play at a time like this.

Six months of dedication, hard work, and mental battles. Though I was still smoking 5 to 6 cigarettes a day, I'll tell you now that I am ashamed to admit this, that's the truth. How I got away with that can only be one reason: power of the mind. Master your mind, and no obstacle will get in your way.

Adam Green the underdog enters the ring first to his song: The Final Countdown in the undercard event.

Here we go, the moment of truth! First round he took full advantage where he came straight at me with an assault. He managed to land a few good shots that seem to have woken me up instantly as my impulse would be to throw a long looping right hand to install my presence. It's the only procedure to do when a boxer has been off for so long. Fuel their weakness and do not even give a chance to think, jump on him right from the start and put the pressure on. This has worked for many in the past. Personally, it just woke me up in a bad way for him. Before that I might have been in the clouds and less focused, but it worked out like it was supposed to, thank you Jesus! I would pass the test Lagrange and I had been working on during training by showing a different Adam Green. Fighting in spots, waiting for proper timing to pop that jab to head and body. Using lateral movements with the mindset of looking good for the judges even though you're supposed to be resting during this time.

Physically, I looked in top shape after 8 years, but I was still "ring rusty". I would give him the 1st round. Round 2 began, and I slowly started to regain my momentum and shake off all the cobwebs. Still showing signs that I wasn't even close to how I usually perform but still getting the job done. I do not know how, but that round became a draw. Round 3 and I feel this is where the bout really starts, where I displayed my new style by loosening up and showing everyone that I'm still walking the walk. Pretty close fight now as I would win the 3rd. On the 4th, I would hurt him and knock him down. I really began marking my territory in round 5 as I would knock him down again, even though the ref would call it a slip. A rule is a rule, I hit him with a straight right-hand and he went down. The ref would call it a slip, and I guess it seemed like my punch wouldn't be hard enough visually. Round 6 and it was a close give and take with an even performance from the both of us. When we came to the center of the ring for the decision to be announced. The emotions were intense, it would be a split decision and the winner... Ladies and gentlemen, would be Adam Green. One of the best highlights of my career. I had good support professionally and personally. I will never forget how Jakob looked at me with tears of happiness in his eyes, showing how proud he was of me, and it touched my heart for life. The people were proud and happy, and I thank them sincerely for being there for their support, their cheers, and to have witnessed the fruit of my life's hard work.

CHAPTER 31: The Price of Passion: Sacrifices for the Boxing Dream.

After the Cotroni fight I took some time off for rest and reflection. My intention was to start back up in September and work in the meantime. The downhill events would unfortunately start here. We had struck a deal with our landlord to square up our debt but move out. Steph and I moved into a friend's apartment down the street from my brother Josh's house. The summer of 2015, Steph and I were not getting along, and I was leaning on alcohol and other substances more than I would have liked. My comeback brought an intense high and purpose in my life, the real-life cost associated with this however was having nowhere to live. These were the risks I was willing to take to pursue my passion and sadly not an uncommon story for many professional fighters out there. Tiffany, on the other hand, had understandably found it difficult and it became the source of a lot of our disagreements.

In August of 2015 we would find our new apartment in the town next to ours called Saint-Louis-de-Gonzague. The calm times allowed us to focus on happiness and were our favorite times together. Jakob and Lohan had their own room when they would come to stay every weekend. As I had mentioned, I greatly enjoyed running and whenever I relocated, I always created running routes for myself to keep in decent condition. I have many running routes, even to this day, maybe too many! Ranging from Hemingford to Chateauguay, Montreal to Victoriaville.

Guylain Ramsey, a businessman with a true passion for boxing, would fancy the idea of Dan Lagrange coming to live in Victoriaville to train their boxers. My idea was instantly to follow Dan. This would destroy Tiffany. Even though I was supposed to come back every weekend it would be too much, and she would not accept this. I received the signal to follow, and I knew this was a good opportunity at 34. I was willing to do anything necessary to achieve my objectives before it became too late. I was very aware that I would not be able to live with myself for the rest of my life, and I'll never wish that on anyone. REGRETS.

I would arrive in Victoriaville on a Sunday evening and remember seeing how happy Dan was when I got there. "Are you ready bitch?" with a big smile on his face. Our training camp would start there. I stayed with Dan who was living with his girlfriend and her son. Everything was set. By Thursday I recall Mr. Ramsey would take me to the garage with my car and give it a tune up, then sign some papers making him my new manager. It looked as if everything was proceeding in the right direction. One day left and then I could go back to see Tiffany, I was constantly thinking of her. To be real I was worried sick.

Friday morning, I would run with my partner named Tommy as he would take me to the ski mountains for an efficient cardio enhancer. Then later in the day, I would do my last training for the week at the boxing gym. Afterwards, I would have supper and hit the road as soon as I could, to head back to Saint-Louis-de-Gonzague to see my Tiffany. It was an emotional drive with every second feeling like an hour. When I arrived and walked up those long staircases to get to the apartment and opened the door, it was a demoralizing sight. Tiffany's aura and visible emotions would not mirror my own. She was sitting on the table just looking down at the floor. There would be no response to my greeting, and it all went downhill from there. I won't get into details, but an argument erupted, screaming at one another. It would finish off by me pulling her hair and pushing her to the ground. I would leave and take off. Our landlord, who lived just below us, had called the cops. I was unaware of this and was considered to be on the run. Back then the only way I knew how to escape was to bury my emotions with drugs and alcohol. I was lost, sad, and confused. I ended up sleeping at a friend's house that night.

When I woke up that morning, I was an absolute mess with only one thing on my mind: Tiffany. That night would end up with me going back to Saint-Louis-de-Gonzague drunk out of my mind. I was desperate with a one-track thought and got to the apartment and looked all over for Tiffany with no luck. Down the street, there would be a bar and I felt at the time that would be my solution. I left the bar late that night, and Steph was nowhere to be found. Out of desperation I had the idea of going back to my dad's house. It would be a little difficult since it would not be the same as if my dad had a new girlfriend, however it wouldn't matter because the police pulled me over. They had observed me swerve all over the road and wouldn't feel the need to give me a breathalyzer as they could clearly see what condition I was in. At the time I naively believed I was cool by showing them my last fight on YouTube against Cotroni. I would be on my way to jail once again. Talk about an attitude adjustment! This would be a wakeup call for me as I woke up in a holding cell, to realize that I was being transferred to Bordeaux Prison. God was with me there and would be my savior as I most definitely needed the help and guidance. My comeback trial would be put back on hold. I spent a few nights in jail. They would give me an option to go to therapy for drinking and I immediately took advantage of the opportunity to receive some much-needed help without hesitation. During my first night, I was placed in a holding cell for 24 hours. That was a significant test right from the start, then I would be allowed in the jail grounds. Honestly, it's hard to write about this messed up part of my life, but it's reality.

September 2015, I was driven to L'Envolee Therapy Centre outside of Granby Quebec to start my recovery. After a week or so there, I was playing in a soccer game and a player missed the ball and kicked my shin bone that put me in a wheelchair. I was at the end of my limit for patience. After one month, they discussed putting me on a trial run to see if therapy had made its progress. I was allowed to leave for a weekend, but I'd be coming back to be put through tests to see if I am using drugs or alcohol. I was doing my best to pay close attention during class because I was truly serious in receiving all the help that they were giving me. I didn't want to waste any time, I had to get better. My father and his girlfriend would come to visit me, they would bring my boy Jakob alongside them. Every time they came, we would play my favorite board game of all time: monopoly. I was truly blessed but at the same time my mental state would be in a bad condition with constantly thinking about Tiffany. I had found out that she was now living at my supposedly good friend's house, and they were now together. With everything going on this was a tough one to swallow. It shook me up and it literally stole my breath away. I felt as if life was throwing me test after test. I can easily say it was the top three of the hardest times in my life. To make things even worse I would recall I had been talking to Steph and she was supposed to visit me one Sunday... but never came.

Finally! I was allowed to go to the outer world for a weekend. Everything had to be arranged to ensure there were no temptations or plans to consume any alcohol or drugs. Like most things in life, it's best to have a strategy, just like when you prepare for a fight. Life can feel like endless battles at times but what doesn't break you can only make you better if you decide to make the right decisions during the toughest moments. It honestly was a relief for my soul knowing I had people who loved and cared for me. I stayed at my father's house for that weekend, and I would still have my driving license. I took the opportunity the first night to see my old best friend Jeff just to hang out. Little did I know that Jeff had set up a blind date for me and brought me to her house. This was a little difficult, as in the past I always used alcohol to help ease any tension or nerves I would have during a first date. After what I had been through, I was more than good without any intoxicants. As soon as I woke up, she was offering me breakfast and coffee but all I wanted was to see and talk with Tiffany and ended up leaving a short while after. Later in the day at my dad's, I decided to call Steph and coincidentally she would be on her way to see me. When she arrived, my father would be skeptical and would ask her some questions just to make sure it was in my best interest if she was to see me. After hours of talking things through and sorting out some issues I was back with my love.

Sunday came and I was to be back in Granby by 7pm. Steph drove me back but would have nowhere to stay. My beloved Auntie Marielle (one of my dad sisters) who lives in Montreal generously offered to allow Steph to temporarily stay with her. The weekend couldn't have gone much better.

CHAPTER 32: A Rocky Road to Recovery: Struggles and Setbacks

I spent 3 and a half months in that place as well as celebrating my 35th birthday. I would put myself in decent condition with the help of some of the people I had met in therapy by shadow boxing and lots of laps around the building. Unfortunately, I had a dispute with one of the other residents and ended up saying things that would be considered threatening resulting in my expulsion from the program. Seeing that I was 35 and the program was supposed to last 6 months, I wanted to prioritize focusing on my boxing career. I knew I had no time to waste. So, I was to head back to jail to await trial. The good news was I didn't have to go back to that holding cell for 24 hours straight. I would go to trial and receive an order to be dismissed on the alternative to go to a 3-week therapy at *Maison La Margelle* in Sorel, Quebec in March. We would be at the end of January, and I was to stay sober till then. A blessing for me to pursue my objective in my life.

Steph and I didn't have a place to stay once I got out so I'm going to thank my boy Mr. Jeff Saumier for letting us stay with him and his family until we could figure something out. In March 2016, I headed to *Maison La Margelle* in Sorel-Tracy. This would be a walk in the park as there were no inmates that were present in this picture. The rumor of Dan Lagrange being back in Valleyfield gave me the impression that everything seemed to be working out in the proper manner. I completed my 3-week program with ease near the end of March. Now that I was clean and sober, I would be back on my mission with nothing slowing me down except for still smoking 5 cigarettes a day. One vice at a time, but the worst ones were behind me. Back at it with my man Dan Lagrange and now I would be training at the new boxing club in Valleyfield called *Viking*.

Now eventually with time, Steph and I would find a place to stay in a room at this nice lady's house, her name was Brenda Elder. She was a naturalist, and truly good person that we were blessed to have crossed paths with. I would also like to take the time to THANK YOU for all you have done for us.

My next opponent was the up-and-comer Louisbert Altidore. The contract would be set for 4 rounds, and I'd receive a purse of $4000. I didn't agree with the 4 round part as I felt I was going back down since my last fight was 6 rounds. Louisbert was undefeated in three fights and the weight would be set at 165 pounds. Once again, I would be considered the underdog. Not a problem really, however Dan would be a little worried on the fact I didn't do a whole lot of quality sparring for this fight, most likely due to the fact both of us didn't have driving licenses anymore. I would compromise by sparring with heavyweights in which I would receive

some big shots that could have done some damage. I could have just used my boxing skills and schooled them; however, my ignorant head decided to play tough guy and go to war instead. To be straight, at the time I had the impatient thoughts of *"let's do it now, I don't have any time to waste"*. Though Dan was concerned about my head, I was really concerned about my age factor and an easy

4g's underestimated the 4-round part and potential injury. That was my mentality for this fight.

Now my training would be a totally different aspect in the sense that I believed at the time that everything had to move fast. I was determined, as the last time I did a 4 rounder was in 2003. The date would be set for May 13, 2016, at club Metropolis. This would be the first fight where Jeff would work in my corner with Lagrange, and experience what it's like in between the rounds.

1st round I started way too fast, as you could say I underestimated a 4-round fight. I didn't have any control of my emotions, that's a no-no for boxing since by round 3 I was near the end and fighting on fumes. This fight I would still be smoking 5 cigarettes a day. I'm in total disbelief and ashamed to tell you this today. Its facts and I would lose to the upcomer Altidor by decision.

To put the icing on the cake, the next day in the hotel, we were in bad shape from getting intoxicated and feeling rough and depressed. Steph and I would be awakened rudely by Dan saying that he couldn't find his glasses. I lost patience instantaneously. We would have a battle in the hotel room, and Steph would witness it all, poor her. That would be the end for us. Training goals would no longer be in the picture. I honestly thought *"ok that's it. I'm done. Fuck it! I'm hanging them up... again"*.

CHAPTER 33: Twist of fate: A Message from a Matchmaker.

As time went on, I worked for my father and big bro Josh, until the end of November then collected unemployment for the winter. Steph and I seemed to be coming to an end, once again, as her mom came to pick her up along with her belongings.

Still living at Brenda's on the 138, I recall we would discuss life, looking for a little direction. I was lost and I'll never forget she was on her computer talking with me, as I was scrolling on my phone, looking at old messages. Danny Mcgarvie a well-known Canadian boxing matchmaker from Vancouver had sent me a message request that I hadn't seen until now it:

Danny McGarvie, May 22, 2016: "Adam I'm a matchmaker based out of Vancouver, do you want to fight in June? 4 or 6 rounds. Do you have a manager you want me to talk to?"

May 25, 2016 "Adam I have a great opportunity to fight a major belt & a WBU eliminator world title. Are you sure you don't want to talk?"

Adam, Dec 5,2016: "Hey, I just seen this message now, wtf"

Danny, Dec 5, 2016: "That was a long time ago, but here's my number-"

MAY 22, 2016 AT 2:27 P.M.

Adam I am a matchmaker based out of Vancouver , do you want to fight in June

4 or 6 rounds

do you have a manager you want me to talk to

MAY 25, 2016 AT 12:58 P.M.

Adam I have a great opportunity to fight for a major belt & a WBU eliminator world title are you sure you don't want to talk

DEC 5, 2016 AT 5:27 P.M.

Hey i just seen this message now wtf

That was a long time ago

May

I c

I was talking about you today and a few times

DEC 5, 20   5:49 P.M.

After we spoke on the phone, he said there was an opportunity to fight the current

Canadian middleweight champion Paul Bzdel in two months. This happened because Cotroni had fought him and lost by decision in October 2016. This is how the opportunity fell on my lap.

Now I had to move quickly and find a trainer. I kept hearing about all the success of my old training partner back in 2004 Ian Mackillop who was now training a prominent contender named Shakel Phinn, who actually fought Bzdel himself for the Canadian super middleweight title Feb 27th, 2016, in Saskatoon. Phinn would win by decision and was now the Canadian Super Middleweight Champ. I would receive the ok from Ian to come and train with them at Donnybrook Boxing Gym in Verdun, Montreal. I needed a place to stay in the city and immediately thought of dear auntie Marielle.

Everything seemed to be arranged, my father would still work on the odd day when the weather was ok for us during wintertime. He would take me to the side and say, "Adam don't do it, I saw your last fight, you're not the same." Now perhaps he was right according to my agility and speed. He wouldn't be aware of the burning desire I still had. There was no way I was passing up this opportunity. This is it I'm really going to give it my best shot and that's it. I know dad you care for my health. Thank you but I'm an adult with my own ideas. My aunt would come and pick me up at Brenda's with all my stuff. We would make a little stop at the IGA in Ormstown. I had the idea of quitting smoking, then made it into a reality. This is it; I'm going to the pharmacy to try nicotine gum. It worked like a charm "*good move Adam! proud of me*" my mind was aligned with my goals. I quit all my bad habits, and I would acquire all the door openers that were needed to conquer my destination.

I was making all the right decisions. Of course, in the back of my mind I would have my doubts "*maybe dad was right. Mind over matter Adam, you can do it champ!*" The first person I would communicate with, when I got to Montreal, would be Manny Montreal. He is a boxing analyst, and he would give me directions on how to get around using public transit and would provide me with a conditioning gym that his brother owned in Lasalle called Prestige Fitness. They helped me till the end of my career as I had another 2 fights after this one. Thank you, Manny, I hope you and your brother are reading this! The two of you are truly wonderful people!! I'll never forget about you, my man; may God bless you and your brother as well. Straight up love you guys' MANNY MONTREAL and ROB MARTINEZ.

All up to me now, the moment of truth is on its way. Make it count every single day, no excuse for nothing. I talked the talk and now I would have to walk a long walk, day in, day out every single day would matter. I knew of Paul Bzdel, and I think he's a real true passionate fighter. I do not say that about more than half of any of the boxers, especially to this day. It could be that I'm particular, however I would rather stay true to my feelings.

Initially what I thought was a setback was actually a blessing. The fight was now postponed until April 29th. Everything happens for a reason. As I mentioned earlier, I had a setback with Desormiers in 2006. When the fight was postponed, I took it like a setback, now I knew this was the signal to put myself in tip-top-peaking-perfect-physical condition and most important mentally. Now God granted me with more time to do whatever needs to be done to achieve my success. Time was on my side now.

My training schedule was to be at Donnybrook for 10 am, train approximately 2 hrs still using my most important tool, a small meal every 2 hours. I would have everyone there that I needed "A" class professionals, and a trainer who knew exactly what to do in preparing for a championship fight. During the week of training, I would have to use my experience, if not you, will be burnt out by Wednesday. Immediately after training I would replenish my body with fruits and take the bus back to my aunt's. There I would have all my meals prepared and portioned in advance. When eating every 2 hours, that's indeed a necessity, always talking for myself, so I would have my meal include lean protein, complex carbohydrates, and tons of veggies. Fruit for dessert and a tall glass of fresh water. After I would take a walk, after kicking my legs and moving my arms to help release the tension, avoid stiffness, and assist digestion of that small meal I just put in me. A nice stretch. Then I would take a good hour nap, eat, and then prepare my training gear and ammunition (food) to bring with me to Prestige fitness in LaSalle. Rob Montreal would be there, and he would supply me with all kinds of natural products, before and after training with the goal of decreasing my weight. He would even grant me with my own conditioning coach named Salomon Torabi.

In between my training, I always made sure I had time for my boy Jakob who was on the verge of turning 10. I'd make a point of attending his karate classes every Thursday in Chateauguay, where he would be quite successful in winning titles across the world. Caroline was now married to a karate sensei, and that's where I would go to see him at his class. We would usually play chess and go to the park and have some fun together. And when Friday had come, I would take a bus back to my hometown, to visit the girl I was in love with. We were still communicating everyday though it was tough for the both of us. She would now be living with her parents down in Dundee near the

Quebec-US border. She would come to pick me up in Ormstown where the bus would drop me off. Really, we didn't have anywhere to go after, it wouldn't really be a factor as both of us were happy just to spend time together. My goal was to recuperate by Monday. On Saturday I would take an extended light run. Sunday would be my full day of rest not moving a muscle and that night I would go back to Montreal, to my wonderful auntie Marielle's home and prepare for the long tough week ahead.

It was a blessing to have auntie Marielle as she's my savior. She was friends with my grandpa Jim. Grandpa had a friend named Slim; ironically, he was a German soldier as my grandpa was Jewish. As crazy as it sounds, they would all be friends. They would often play cards, chat, and sometimes there would even be a little arguing that took place, due to their different opinions.

I really did everything for this fight, apart from the fact I would take a couple puffs of a joint. On Saturday, I would indulge in a special wine that didn't have any effects on my weight. I was part of a group called Smart Recovery that would meet in Upper Lachine and there would coincidently be an old friend from back in the day. That took place every Wednesday night. For 3 months of this, I had a schedule to follow which kept me regimented. I put everything on the line. At the time, I felt good and at peace as I truly did everything in my power to better myself. I was really well prepared for this fight; I had access to top quality sparring, an experienced trainer, and a conditioning gym. I was blessed and now it was all up to me to deliver.

Publication de Ian MacKillop

 Ian MacKillop est avec **Adam Green** à **Winnipeg Richardson International Airport**.
27 avril 2017 · Winnipeg, Manitoba

On our way to Saskatoon for Adams Canadian Title fight!!

Finn Macfarlane, Arley Whyte et 160 autres — 52 commentaires

👍 J'aime — 💬 Commenter

Plus pertinents ▾

Alvin Tam
Come visit me here in calgary coach.. lols.
7 a · J'aime · Répondre

CHAPTER 34: Manifesting Dreams into Reality: Mind Over Matter.

I would fly into Paul Bzdel's hometown of Saskatoon, Saskatchewan, on April 27th with Ian McKillop. We arrived there in the late afternoon; our idea was to have a little something to eat at the airport. I would be a few pounds over, which was reasonable as I still had approximately 12 hours until the weigh-in. An important factor to mention is that every scale is a little different, but the official scale is the only one that counts.

On the morning of the 28th, I was edgy and a little impatient since the weigh-in would be held at 6pm, so timing comes into play. The primary goal is to make the weight while not becoming too weak in the process. I felt dull with low energy; however, it wouldn't be my first time doing this and I was aware of how I felt during this difficult requirement. For some boxers, making weight is the most crucial part of this game, myself included. I'm talking about the months of reaching top physical condition while respecting the weight that you signed for.

Ian and I had a game plan and we followed it with perfect timing. I lost my last pounds in a sauna, then without waiting we headed to the official weigh-in. I'm very fortunate to have had the opportunity to have Mr. Ian McKillop by my side as my coach as he had a toolbox of tricks and tips that he had gained as a veteran boxer himself. I was in good hands and because of him, I would feel at ease and confident. As soon as I got off the scale with success, I would immediately replenish with Pedialyte water, fruits, and then my favorite pre-fight food, a steak meal. Then it was time for total recuperation centered around ice baths. I recall how good I felt talking with Ian and Danny Mac at the hotel. It felt like I was ready for the most important fight of my life.

My mind would be at ease, and I would sleep like a baby. There were many fights where I got 2 to 3hrs of sleep due to thoughts and nerves. Bottom line, before you close your eyes to sleep, make sure your mind is functioning in proper fashion, otherwise it will be a long sleepless scary night. It looked like everything was perfect. When we arrived at the venue, I checked my fight bag and realized that I forgot my fucking mouthpiece!! It was roughly a 10-minute drive and it would be the longest 20 minutes of my life. My thoughts were racing. "*GET A HOLD OF YOURSELF, YOU CAN DO IT CHAMP! THIS*

IS IT!".

When I was to warm up with Ian again, I would be a little stiff and tight. Danny Mac would take a little video that would go on to social media.

The moment of truth had arrived.

Distractions will inevitably arise before a fight but what makes champions is the power of the mind. Not letting any incident distract you at any given moment especially before a fight.

Going into that fight I might have lost the first couple of rounds, but it would truly appear as if it was my time to shine, since styles make fights and Bzdel suited my style. Don't get me wrong, he would be able to catch me with a few good shots and rumour would be that he was ahead on the scorecards even though his face was a bloody mess. Styles end up complementing other styles and you could say Bzdel would be a match for me. I feel horrible for the massacre I put to him, but this was for the national title, no holding back. Respectfully, Paul Bzdel could quite possibly be the nicest person I have ever encountered in the ring. I knocked him down twice and the second time when he rose from the mat, the ref counted to 8, looked at Bzdel straight in his eyes and said "that's it" waving his arms and thus signaling my hard-earned victory. There it was, perhaps took me months to realize what I had just accomplished, but everything was right there: dedication, commitment, mental and physical pain. Constant repetition over and over, never surrendering had all finally paid off. I remember truly envisioning this scene that just occurred, over, and over and over in my mind till I made it into a reality that night! April 29th, 2017, was the most successful day of my life marking me down in Canadian history as the 2017 MIDDLEWEIGHT CHAMPION! WOW!

What a turnaround compared to my first attempt to be the Canadian Champion back in 2005 against Victor Lupu. I failed because I never manifested the victory by making the proper image in my mind, months before the fight.

In hindsight, the journey to becoming a Champion is grander than the title itself. When I add together all the literal blood, sweat, tears, sacrifices, wins, and losses- all the countless hours of building muscle memory, kilometers ran, sleepless nights, financial stress, personal traumas, and the fucking dieting; the title of Champion is it's own crown of thorns that a certain few wear not to show greatness but rather a dedication to something grander than themselves. Believe in your dreams and make it true with your actions.

Power of the mind.

CONCLUSION

About one month after my fight vs Paul BZDEL. David Whittom my former training partner was attempting to conquer the super middleweight Canadian Title vs Heavy Hands Gary Kopas this tragedy was an abslout nightmere as David would go to the hospital after the fight as he wasn't feeling well, would slip into a coma n would never get out of it. Just to revel how dangerous this sport can be, this would not be the first time something like this would happen in this sport. Steph n I would come to an end once again in august of 2024 n this time we would not come back together. We had our daughter Miley in December of 2019 broke up 4 or 5 times since then went through a lot of drama n BS n ended up loosing her in 2022. Shes in a goods hands, however one day shes coming back with me n I wont stop til she does. I was able to regain my lisence after 7 n half years, as in 2022 I would go to anther therapy n I had the counselor help me n I would to thank Ludivic right here as he would be indeed a blessing to have crossed paths with. After I retired in December of 2017.Iwas able to get a job on the 22nd of Feberary 2018 that I still have to this day, in April of 2024 I would stop working basically for to reasons when I moved to vallyfied in March 2018 I moved into a room n next to would b my friend for the next 6 years named Julien Chernard past away in February 2024 n also I was going threw health issues I had an operation to try in fix things but it only made my issue a lot more problematic n still battling to this day every single day is a nightmere as I believe God is putting me threw the hardest test ive ever been through.

Im sure your all aware that I never give up, n I will fight right until the end of time. I Like to all a happy life n to enjoy all that God gives to you, n to thank each and everyone who took the time to read my book. GOD BLESS N THANKS TO ALL.

www.ingramcontent.com/pod-product-compliance
Lightning Source LLC
Chambersburg PA
CBHW052032070526
44584CB00016B/2013